A CONCISE HISTORY OF THE UNITED STATES

Prom.Lupi

Portus Regalis, ſiue F. S. Helenæ.

5

A CONCISE HISTORY OF THE

UNITED
STATES

ANDREW SINCLAIR

with 240 illustrations

A STUDIO BOOK
THE VIKING PRESS
NEW YORK

For Mrs Patrick Eve

Frontispiece: Jean Ribaut's expedition in 1562
to what is now South Carolina.

ACKNOWLEDGEMENTS
The author acknowledges with thanks the kind permission of Random House,
Inc., to quote from Archibald MacLeish's *Brave New World* and of Holt,
Rinehart and Winston, Inc., to quote from Robert Frost's *The Gift Outright*.

Published in 1967 by the Viking Press, Inc.
625 Madison Avenue, New York, N.Y. 10022
Printed in Great Britain by Jarrold and Sons Ltd, Norwich, England

Contents

If we seek examples for our country and for ourselves, let us resort to the new-created West. There the fountains are uncorrupted. There civilization meets nature unimpaired. There we can behold how the young armed American grapples with the wilderness, and thence we can return and imagine how our fathers lived. Europe presents much to our view, but America still more. . . .

We can do much for Europe by doing more for ourselves. We must perfect our system, and show what liberty is worth: we must convince the rich and the poor that it is the fountain of justice, the source of prosperity, the safeguard of the citizen, and the foundation of National Perfection.

WILLIAM F. OTIS, 1831

Indians. Watercolour by John White, who was sent by Queen Elizabeth I as draughtsman to Sir Walter Raleigh's second expedition to Virginia in 1585.

Chapter One

In the beginning, America was a continent, set between the Atlantic and Pacific Oceans, divided into two parts by a narrow isthmus, a North America and a South America. Two great rivers and two great ranges of mountains were to be vital in the history of the North: the St Lawrence which joined the Atlantic to the Great Lakes and the Mississippi which joined them to the Caribbean; the Appalachian Mountains which rose like a stockade behind the eastern seaboard and the Rocky Mountains which rose like towers behind the western seaboard.

Outside of Mexico and Peru, the tribes of Indians who first existed in this vast mass of land were scattered sparsely across the prairies and the forests, and, in the cold regions of the Arctic, men were as rare as game above the ice. The first Europeans to reach America, the Norsemen, died of the winter, for nature was the ruler of the earth and there was no appeal to other men. At the time of the landing of Columbus, perhaps 500,000 Indians lived in all the continent above the Rio Grande, a handful of tribes at war with one another, living uneasily on the abundant produce of the wilderness.

When Columbus discovered the New World for Spain in 1492, he was searching for a *new* world to discover. He was a Utopian, and he described his explorations in terms of the dreams of the European mind. His letter to King Ferdinand and Queen Isabella after his third voyage talks of an 'earthly paradise' near the Orinoco River, and his journal is full of the chant of nightingales (which do not exist in the Americas), of everlasting spring, of green trees, and of innocent and noble savages. The New World was 'a land to be desired, and, once seen, never to be left'.

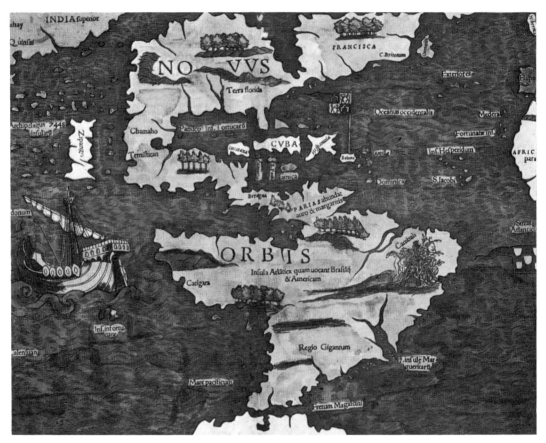

One of the earliest maps of America was Sebastian Münster's *Novus Orbis*, 1540. The first version of the map (without the ship) appeared in 1532, forty years after Columbus landed in the West Indies.

Yet Columbus had meant to find China; his discovery of the Americas was less an advantage to him than an obstacle. The Orient was cut off from Europe by this new continent, which passed under the control of Spain by the Treaty of Tordesillas in 1494. By this treaty, which split the unknown world between Spain and Portugal, Spain took the West and most of the Americas while Portugal took the East and the Spice Islands; a later treaty extended Spanish influence as far as the Philippine Islands. The discovery of the gold of Mexico and the silver of Peru compensated the Spaniards for the loss of the silk and spice trade to Portugal – a country which they were soon to absorb. Their plunder of the Aztec and Inca empires allowed them to finance a war of conquest in Europe that lasted for a century. The abundance of the New World, for the first of many times, was used to intervene in the wars of the Old.

Christopher Columbus.
This possibly authentic portrait
is attributed to
Ridolfo Ghirlandaio.

The Franciscan mission
of San Estévan in Ácoma,
New Mexico, built
c. 1642. In spite of the
advantage Columbus had
given them, the Spanish
were poor colonists.
Though by 1624 there
were 20 friars, 43 churches
and 34,000 Christian In-
dians in New Mexico,
even at the end of the
century there were still
only 2000 Spanish settlers.

An Indian village and Indians fishing. Two watercolours by John White 1585-7.

Since the Spaniards seemed to have found El Dorado, if not Eden, on the other side of the Atlantic, the sea-faring countries of Europe followed them to the Americas. The human sacrifices of the Aztecs, the tortures inflicted by some Indian tribes on their prisoners, and the promiscuity and nakedness in which most of the Indians lived soon changed the explorers' picture of the Noble Savage to that of the savage, pure and unadorned. The innocence of the New World remained only a legend to attract immigrants from the Old; the occasional brutality of the Indian was a constant fear to European pioneers and gave them an excuse to enslave or massacre the first inhabitants of the Americas. The Spaniards put the natives by their millions to work until death in the mines, while the practice of scalping was introduced to many Indian tribes by French and English backwoodsmen; missionaries also brought in the idea of crucifixion – a torture which the Indians found suitable for the enemies they could not forgive.

Spanish influence on South and Central America remained dominant until the twentieth century; but in the North the French, the English, and the Dutch came in search of fish and furs. The French used the St Lawrence and the Mississippi in a great strategic plan to dominate the fur trade of the northern continent by a system of forts and Indian alliances along the two vital rivers. Their forts kept the interloping English and Dutch penned along a narrow coastal strip stretching from Nova Scotia to Georgia, while the Spanish held the Caribbean coast from Florida to Mexico.

In fact, the Spaniards and the French first set the American pioneer tradition of westering. Cabeza de Vaca, who reached the borders of Arizona and New Mexico in 1536 along with the Negro Estéban, wrote: 'We ever held it certain that going towards the sunset we would find what we desired.' Coronado, the conqueror, followed after de Vaca to plunder the legendary Cíbola five years later; he found only the seven pueblo cities of the Zuñi Indians, unquestionably the most developed urban civilization on the whole North American continent at that time; but the Zuñis were rich only in grain and dignity and peace and arts rather than in gold. 'Granted that they did not find the riches of which they had been told,' one of Coronado's men wrote of his companions, 'they found a place in which to search for them, and the beginning of a good country to settle in, so as to go farther from there.' The Spaniards, indeed, went farther west and left colonies and missions as far as California.

The Hopi pueblo of Walpi, Arizona. Coronado sent Pedro de Tovar here after he had taken Cíbola in 1540 without finding any sign of the legendary treasure.

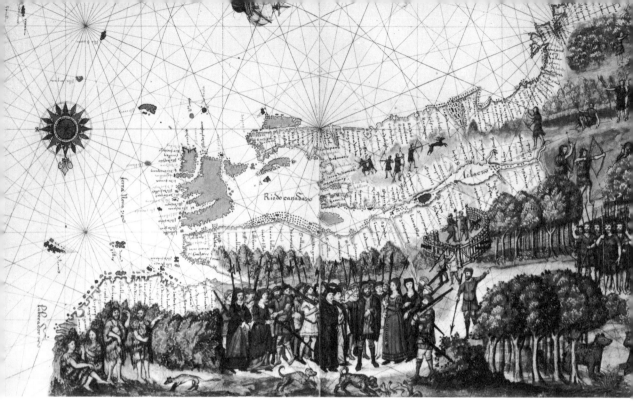

Though Jacques Cartier landed at Gaspé in 1534, the French made no real attempt to establish an empire there till the next century.

The French trappers and Jesuits also pushed beyond the Great Lakes into the Northwest. The French had been the first to refuse to recognize the Treaty of Tordesillas. In 1523, a French pirate had intercepted some of the treasure ships bringing back the gold of the Aztec emperor, Montezuma, to Spain. When the Spaniards protested, the King of France kept the treasure and replied: 'Show me the clause in Adam's will by which he divided the world between my brothers of Spain and Portugal.' Thereafter, Verrazano and Cartier explored the North American coast and the St Lawrence for France, while the great Champlain set up a French fur empire on the St Lawrence. An alliance was formed with the Huron Indians; the Jesuits and the fur-traders were used as the instruments of French expansion. Father Marquette and Joliet were the first Europeans to float down the Mississippi almost as far as the delta, and eventually, after La Salle's brilliant exploration of the river, the French founded New Orleans in 1718 to dominate the mouth of the Mississippi and complete their grand design of controlling the American West.

Between the two great continental rivers lay the new English and Dutch colonies of the Atlantic seaboard; for the success of the Spanish and the French in the New World had brought over their European enemies. The first English colony was founded by Captain John Smith and others in swampy Jamestown, Virginia, in 1607. It prospered initially more in legend than in fact, even if Virginia was later to become the leading American state in the years after the American Revolution. The legend of Pocahontas as the saviour of the gallant Captain Smith's life from her Indian tribe was probably a later invention by the Captain; the Indian princess herself, later glorified as dignified and innocent, was described by her English husband as 'one whose education hath been rude, her manners barbarous, her generation accursed'. Once again the myth of the Noble Savage contradicted the experience of those who lived with the savage. Yet, the myth of gold had brought the English to the bogs of Virginia in the first place; there was, Captain Smith complained, 'no talk, no hope, no work, but dig gold, wash gold, refine gold, load gold'. Until the shrewd discovery that tobacco, grown by Negro slaves, was as good as gold and that slaves breeding slaves were black gold coining black gold, the colony of Virginia seemed likely to be no more than a malarial nightmare.

Captain John Smith

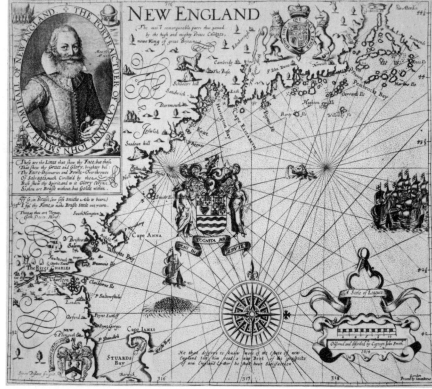

The only known likeness of Captain John Smith is an inset to this map from his *A Description of New England*, published in 1616. Smith saved Jamestown, but the legend of Pocahontas (*above*) is now thought to have been largely his own invention.

Plymouth, where the Pilgrims landed on 22 December 1620, was so named by Captain John Smith in 1614 (see map on p. 15).

The Pilgrim
Fathers

The *Mayflower* landed the Pilgrims at Plymouth in 1620; but the colony there barely survived. More important was the landing of the *Arbella* in Boston Bay ten years later. By the end of the year, a flourishing colony of two thousand immigrants had been established; it soon absorbed the struggling Pilgrims inside the new Commonwealth of Massachusetts. Nothing can be more eloquent of the speed and the spirit with which the Puritans set up their good life in the New World than the simple description of the founding of Harvard College in the mere seventh year of the new colony. 'After God had carried us safe to *New England*, and we had builded our houses, provided necessaries for our livelihood, reared convenient places for God's worship, and settled the civil government: One of the things we looked for, and looked after was to advance *Learning* and perpetuate it to Posterity.' Such rapid progress showed a revolutionary urge to construct from nothing a society for the moment and for ever.

The rigour of the wilderness forced the resourceful into a race against time, if they were to preserve any form of civilization on the rim of barbarism. The immediate temptation of virgin land and savage life outside the tiny area of European settlement provoked a counter-attack of moralism. The harshness of the Calvinists, indeed, was born in their own sufferings at the hands

The Jonathan Fairbanks house (*left*) at Dedham, Massachusetts, built *c.* 1636, is thought to be the oldest surviving frame house in America. Harvard, the oldest university (*below*), also dates back to 1636.

Auction handbill.

Anglo-French
Rivalry

of Englishmen and nature; but Calvinism succeeded in New England for two centuries because it was the creed that held together the ruling groups among the immigrants, threatened by Indians and wilderness and sea and inward temptation. Once the frontier had been pushed back beyond the Ohio Valley and Indian raids were no nearer than a grandfather's tale, the rock of Calvinism was weathered into a smoother stone of religion. It was no longer then the bastion of civilization, but its comfort.

American life never forgot the Puritans. Although few in number, they dominated New England when it was the richest and most populated area in North America. Pioneers from New England settled the Ohio Valley and the Middle West; other Puritans led American literature and education until this century. In fact, the reason for some American laws and much American culture is still to be found in the byways of the Calvinist conscience. Morality and religion, democracy and government were all affected by the Puritans; to this day the wide gap between myth and practice in the United States reflects the frustrated hope of the Calvinists that they would found a City of God on the Atlantic coast, not the Megalopolis of Mammon. The Puritans tried as hard as any dedicated group of revolutionaries to house their idealism in bricks; their legacy, along with that of the Quakers of Nantucket and Pennsylvania, has been the remnants of the Yankee spirit, independent, proud, honest, God-fearing, adventurous, inventive, self-controlled, and a little dull. If the proper study of mankind is man, the proper study of the roots of the American is the Puritan.

While the English built up their colonies along the Atlantic, they also tried to outflank the French control of the St Lawrence. A French explorer of Hudson Bay, finding no French patrons, turned over his knowledge to the English. They set up the Hudson's Bay Company, which sought after the elusive Northwest Passage to China and found Indian allies in the Northwest, at the backs of the French, in order to steal the fur trade from their rivals.

The English were lucky to have the aggressive Iroquois as their allies against the French, who had offended the Iroquois by siding with their traditional enemies, the Hurons. The competition of the English and the French in North America was made bloodier by the use of Indian mercenaries to massacre each other. For the British were determined to destroy the French forts on the St Lawrence and to link their outposts on Hudson Bay with the Atlantic colonies.

The Hudson's Bay Company, whose charter (*below left*) was granted in 1670, came to dominate Canada. Though allied to the powerful Iroquois (the two right-hand figures of the Indian group), the English settlers still built strongholds like Fort Nelson (*above*), not only against hostile Indians, such as the Algonquin (on the left of the Indian group), but also, as in this case, against the French.

The Dutch, however, founded their own colony of New Amsterdam on the site of New York. This selection of the best natural harbour on the Atlantic, with its pass through the mountains towards the Great Lakes along the course of the Hudson and Mohawk Rivers, gave the Dutch an alternative route to the interior, free from the ice that made the St Lawrence useless in winter. New Amsterdam also had the advantage of splitting the English Atlantic colonies in half; an alliance between the French and the Dutch would have ruined English chances in the New World. But luckily for the English, New Amsterdam fell to them as the spoils of war in 1664, and was renamed New York.

Yet the English colonies of the North and the South remained split from one another by climate, temperament, habit, and way of life. The climate was the most important discord: the hardness of winter and mild summer of the Yankee North, with its rocky soil that drove its settlers to seek their fortune on the sea through trade; the mild winter and miasmal summer of the South, which encouraged its settlers to imitate tropical patterns and import indentured labour – and later slaves – to till the soil. In the northern states, as the French aristocrat de Tocqueville was to note, 'everything was grave, serious, and solemn; it seemed created to be the domain of intelligence, as the South was that of sensual delight'.

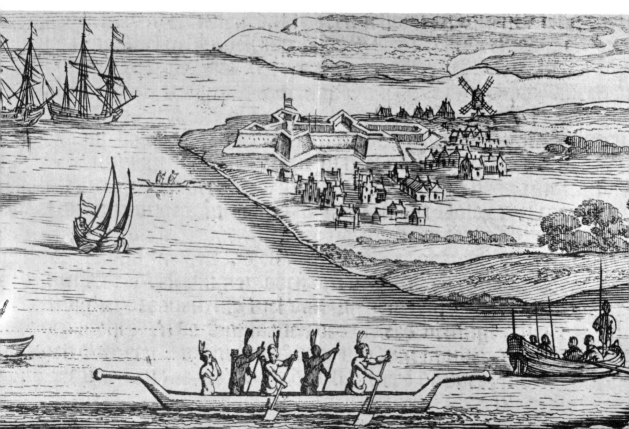

The wealth of the New World was paid for in innocent lives. The *conquistadores* (*left*) used slave labour in the gold mines and the English slavers (*right*) sold their human cargoes to work on sugar, rice, indigo, cotton and tobacco plantations.

Slavery

Although early New England was less puritanical than myth makes out and the southern colonies were more puritanical, yet the Calvinistic business, man or preacher was the ideal of the North, while the gentleman planter was the ideal of the South. By choice, too, the Virginians deliberately produced a master class, entirely dependent on slave labour; by 1724, Negro slaves outnumbered the whites in South Carolina by two to one; forty years later, slaves were nearly half of the population of Virginia. A planter aristocracy had taken over the government of the South from small landowners by the beginning of the eighteenth century. New England traders had also grown rich by ferrying the slaves, although few Negroes were allowed to live in the North.

The Spaniards had reduced the local population to slavery. The English in America, finding Indians too aggressive and unsuitable as labour, had imported Negro prisoners from Africa; the planters in the Caribbean islands had set the example. Even the New Englanders saw little hope of expanding fast enough, without slaves, to make a significant impression on the vast lands that extended, according to Indian tales, far beyond the Appalachian Mountains. 'I do not see how we can thrive,' one Puritan wrote to the famous Governor of Massachusetts, John Winthrop, 'until we get into a stock of slaves sufficient to do all our business, for our children's children will hardly see this great Continent filled with people.'

◀ Earliest known view of New Amsterdam, 1651. The director-general of the Dutch West India Company lived in this small but important settlement.

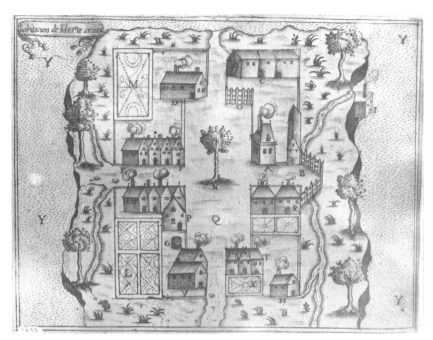

St Croix Island in the Bay of
Fundy, from Champlain's
Voyages, 1613. Champlain
was seeking to found a
settlement here at the time,
so the engraving is
probably idealized.

The very abundance of land made servants hard to find and impossible
to keep. Who would work for another when he could have a farm of his
own? The restricted opportunity of European land allowed the feudal
system; the unlimited acres of the American wilderness liberated both the
greed and the independence of men. The absence of hired hands and the
fertility of virgin soil led to a contradictory solution, democracy for the white
man, because distances were too great from settlement to settlement to allow
strong government, and slavery for the black man, because the Atlantic
passage was the final chain that kept him bound forever to his captors in an
alien land.

Slavery itself did not offend its bloody and violent time; even the Bible
approved of 'the peculiar institution', which seemed a method of 'civilizing'
the Negroes a little by teaching them the virtues of work and Christianity.
And with a desperate shortage of labour, how else was 'the geography of
fantasy' to be made a fact, the fantasy that gave Massachusetts and Connec-
ticut and Virginia and the Carolinas all the land *from sea to sea* westward from
their strip of Atlantic coast? Embedded in the early charters was the idea that
rightfully, despite Indian, Spanish, and French domination of the West, the
continent beyond the Appalachians belonged to the British colonists. Cross
the first mountain barrier – and few suspected that the Pacific lay far beyond
that barrier – and the land was theirs.

So the geography of myth led to the actual geography of European settlement at the time of the struggle of English and French for control of North America. The El Dorados looted by Cortes and Pizarro tempted would-be *conquistadores*, who failed as treasure-seekers, but who opened the way for later settlers. Some of the first explorers in the Americas did get rich quick, as did some of the American pioneers from the gold-mines of the West in the nineteenth century. The myth that gold was for the getting colonized North America at extraordinary speed; even if later immigrants would not expect to plunder or dig gold, they would expect to grow it in grain or acquire it by private industry. The individual greed of men and the dream of instant fortunes exploited and peopled the American wilderness. In the hopeful words of a poem of 1771, another India already existed in the Far West and ships merely had to be sent to the Acapulco coast to return 'laden with pearl and burning gems of gold'.

The first drawing of Niagara Falls, on which this engraving is based, was made by La Salle's chaplain, Father Louis Hennepin, in 1678.

War   The English and the French began an intermittent seventy years' conflict for empire in the 1690s; already, because of the expansion of their sea power, their fighting was world-wide. In North America, their strategy remained consistent. A European quarrel between the founding countries, between Protestant and Catholic, led to a series of raids on each other's outposts. Communications were so bad that large-scale expeditions were nearly impossible; a few hundred European soldiers allied with Indian mercenaries could decide the future of a continent.

In the first fighting, King William's War, the French took over the northern pincer of the British in Hudson Bay. Yet, at the end of the following Queen Anne's War, the English not only regained Hudson Bay, but also annexed Newfoundland and Nova Scotia, which the French had called Acadia, more in hope of its fruitfulness than in observation of its bleakness. The British gains menaced the mouth of the St Lawrence, France's outlet for the fur trade of the interior. Moreover, the Treaty of Utrecht in 1713 recognized the Iroquois as British subjects, giving England a claim to their lands in the Ohio and Mississippi Valleys. The Treaty also gave the British control over the West Indies and the right to open trade with Spanish America – a right which the English navigation laws forbade to Spanish ships in British colonies.

Gaspé had close links with the beginning and the end of France's northern empire. Cartier landed here in 1534 (see p. 14) and General Wolfe lived in the house on the beach in 1759.

In fact, England's triumph in the Americas and rising power in India conjured up a host of envious enemies. By lessening the French and Indian threat to the Atlantic colonies, England was to remove the one fear that kept them quiet under the restrictive commercial laws of the first British Empire – laws that seemed to reserve high profits for English merchants and to deny Americans their favourite liberty, the freedom for any man to gain all he could get and hold. Immediately after Wolfe's decisive battle at Quebec in 1759, which gave England the St Lawrence and the way into the West, the new military governor of the captured fortress reported on the consequences of the victory. '*En bonne politique*', he wrote of Quebec, 'it should perhaps be destroyed, but there may be reasons why it should remain, as it is a guarantee for the good behaviour of its neighbouring colonies.'

Some opposition was, indeed, raised to the British government's insistence on taking over the whole of New France – now called Canada – at the Peace of Paris of 1763; the presence of the French in North America was, in the opinion of one shrewd Duke, 'the greatest security' for the American colonies' dependence on their mother country. By closing their pincers round the St Lawrence, the British made the colonists feel surrounded by no more than the hostile policies of Britain, which now came to play the part of France in the thinking of New England.

The defeat of the French hastened westward expansion by English traders and settlers throughout the North American continent.

LONDON, Published as the Act directs Feb.ᵗ 25 1777 by W.ᵐ FADEN, Corner of S.ᵗ Martin's Lane, Charing-Cross.

The Spanish owned the Mississippi and the West, since the French had ceded their southern possessions and New Orleans to Spain in order to keep them from Britain. And if the English held the land from Hudson Bay down the Atlantic coast as far as the Carolinas, they were confined east of the Mississippi by the huge Spanish area called Louisiana. The new strategy of the aggressive Hudson's Bay Company was to try to extend its penetration in the far North all the way to Oregon, again outflanking the Spanish and their French allies to get at the sources of the fur trade. There they were to meet further competition from the Russian fur-traders, who had crossed the greater distance of Siberia and had reached the Alaskan coasts, sailing across the Bering Straits, where men had probably walked across from Asia to America 11,000 years before.

Early Colonists   In terms of effective occupation, however, European control outside the strip of Atlantic colonies was more a matter of maps than of men on the ground. Claims were much stronger than actual control. The population of all the English colonies on the mainland in 1700 was probably not more than 250,000 people; one-third of these lived in New England and one-quarter in Virginia. Outside the South, travel was possible only eight months a year; since there were few and bad roads, most voyaging was by water, and London was over a month away.

Yet the English were successful as colonists; many men wanted to settle in the New World and a nucleus of flourishing states kept the lines of immigration open. The fertility of the colonists themselves was extraordinary; twenty children in one family was not a rare phenomenon; many mothers had one child in the cradle, one at the breast, and one expected. By the mid-eighteenth century, when the final struggle with the French came, the English colonies contained some 1,300,000 people; this number had nearly doubled by the time of the American Revolution. The attraction of land for the asking drew hordes of dispossessed farmers across the ocean; the Atlantic colonies were so cosmopolitan in the decades before the Revolution that one in three of the white population had been born in a foreign country, and one in four was not of British origin.

The French, however, failed to attract settlers to New France in North America. At the time of the Seven Years War, only 50,000 Frenchmen and their Indian allies stood against England and the colonists. Every expedient was tried to encourage immigration; but the men who arrived in the New World were usually in the fur or fish trade, or in the service of the government,

26

This advice was closer to reality than the normal enthusiastic and totally uninformed emigration tracts. In fact, in 1622 the Indians had all but annihilated the Jamestown settlement, and it was the discovery of a way to cure tobacco and the abolition of a communistic economy which, more than promises of free land, provided the basis for the prosperity of Virginia.

THE INCONVENIENCIES
THAT HAVE HAPPENED TO SOME PERSONS WHICH HAVE TRANSPORTED THEMSELVES

from *England* to *Virginia*, vvithout prouisions necessary to sustaine themselues, hath greatly hindred the *Progresse* of that noble *Plantation*: For preuention of the like disorders heereafter, that no man suffer, either through ignorance or misinformation; it is thought requisite to publish this short declaration: wherein is contained a particular of such necessaries, as either priuate families or single persons shall haue cause to furnish themselues with, for their better support at their first landing in Virginia; whereby also greater numbers may receiue in part, directions how to prouide themselues.

Apparrell.

Apparrell for one man, and so after the rate for more.

	li.	s.	d.
One Monmouth Cap	∞	01	10
Three falling bands		01	03
Three shirts		07	06
One waste-coate		02	02
One suite of Canuase		07	06
One suite of Frize		10	00
One suite of Cloth		15	00
Three paire of Irish stockins		04	
Foure paire of shooes		08	08
One paire of garters		00	10
One doozen of points		00	03
One paire of Canuase sheets		08	00
Seuen ells of Canuase, to make a bed and boulster, to be filled in *Virginia* 8.s. One Rug for a bed 8.s. which with the bed seruing for two men, halfe is		08	00
Fiue ells coorse Canuase, to make a bed at Sea for two men, to be filled with straw, iiij.s.			
One coorse Rug at Sea for two men, will cost vj.s. is for one		05	00
	04	00	00

Victuall.

For a whole yeere for one man, and so for more after the rate.

	li.	s.	d.
Eight bushels of Meale	02	00	00
Two bushels of pease at 3.s.		06	00
Two bushels of Oatemeale 4.s. 6.d.		09	00
One gallon of *Aquauitæ*		02	06
One gallon of Oyle		03	06
Two gallons of Vineger 1.s.		02	00
	03	03	00

Armes.

For one man, but if halfe of your men haue armour it is sufficient so that all haue Peeces and swords.

	li.	s.	d.
One Armour compleat, light		17	00
One long Peece, fiue foot or fiue and a halfe, neere Musket bore	01	02	
One sword		05	
One belt		01	
One bandaleere		01	06
Twenty pound of powder		18	00
Sixty pound of shot or lead, Pistoll and Goose shot		05	00
	03	09	06

Tooles.

For a family of 6. persons and so after the rate for more.

	li.	s.	d.
Fiue broad howes at 2.s. a piece		10	
Fiue narrow howes at 16.d. a piece		06	08
Two broad Axes at 3.s. 8.d. a piece		07	04
Fiue felling Axes at 18.d. a piece		07	06
Two steele hand sawes at 16.d. a piece		02	08
Two two-hand-sawes at 5. s. a piece		10	
One whip-saw, set and filed with box, file, and wrest		10	
Two hammers 12.d. a piece		02	00
Three shouels 18.d. a piece		04	06
Two spades at 18.d. a piece		03	
Two augers 6.d. a piece		01	00
Six chissels 6.d. a piece		03	00
Two percers stocked 4.d. a piece		00	08
Three gimlets 2.d. a piece		00	06
Two hatchets 21.d. a piece		03	06
Two froues to cleaue pale 18.d.		03	00
Two hand-bills 20. a piece		03	04
One grindlestone 4.s.		04	00
Nailes of all sorts to the value of	02	00	00
Two Pickaxes		03	
	06	02	08

Houshold Implements.

For a family of 6. persons, and so for more or lesse after the rate.

	li.	s.	d.
One Iron Pot	00	07	
One kettle		06	
One large frying-pan		02	06
One gridiron		01	06
Two skillets		05	
One spit		02	
Platters, dishes, spoones of wood		04	
	01	08	00

	li.	s.	d.
For Suger, Spice, and fruit, and at Sea for 6. men	00	12	06
So the full charge of Apparrell, Victuall, Armes, Tooles, and houshold stuffe, and after this rate for each person, will amount vnto about the summe of	12	10	
The passage of each man is	06	00	
The fraight of these prouisions for a man, will bee about halfe a Tun, which is	01	10	
So the whole charge will amount to about	20	00	00

Nets, hookes, lines, and a tent must be added, if the number of people be greater, as also some kine.

And this is the vsuall proportion that the Virginia *Company doe bestow vpon their Tenants which they send.*

Whosoeuer transports himselfe or any other at his owne charge vnto *Virginia*, shall for each person so transported before Midsummer 1625. haue to him and his heires for euer fifty Acres of Land vpon a first, and fifty Acres vpon a second diuision.

Imprinted at London by FELIX KYNGSTON. 1622.

and the women were often deported criminals like Manon Lescaut. The French, indeed, made their very lack of numbers and refusal to clear the soil and settle like the English an argument to win over the Indians to their side. Duquesne warned the Iroquois that their allies, the English, would destroy them: 'The forest falls before them as they advance, and the soil is laid bare', while the Indians could hunt up to the very walls of the forts the French had erected.

The Iroquois, by continuing to help the English, did lose their hunting-grounds to them. Pontiac's rebellion of 1763, which harried the frontier towns and farms of the colonies, showed how bitterly the Indians already resented the axes and ploughs of the English. Only the royal proclamation of that same year quieted the Indians a little by reserving for them all the land beyond the sources of the rivers that ran into the Atlantic. This proclamation annoyed the frontier farmers and land speculators, who thought that the government in London was trying to confine them east of the Alleghenies exactly as the French had done, by creating an Indian state around the Great Lakes, which would be a perpetual threat to the restive colonists.

In fact, the colonial policy adopted by the English government was reasonable for its time. England maintained large garrisons in North America to protect the settlers from the French and the Indians; the colonists' own efforts to raise armies for short campaigns had usually been disastrous. In return for this expenditure, England expected to use the colonies as sources of raw

Occasionally contact between Indian and white man was amicable – as when Penn founded Pennsylvania in 1682. Painting by Edward Hicks.

Indians delivering English captives to Colonel Bouquet, 1764. Pontiac's rebellion came to an end at Bushy Run in 1763, and Colonel Bouquet imposed peace terms the following year.

materials and military taxes and as a market for English manufactured goods. A member of the British Board of Trade and Plantations wrote: 'Every act of a dependent provincial government ought therefore to terminate in the advantage of the mother state unto whom it owes its being and protection . . . such is the end of the colonies, and if this use cannot be made of them it will be much better for the state to do without them.'

The remoteness of America from England, the distance from state to state and from town to town, and human fallibility made impossible the consistent administration of the British colonial laws. The Americans were not meant to deal directly with the West Indies or Africa; to make up their adverse balance of trade with England, they had to get cash from exporting elsewhere or from privateering. The southern states, which exported raw materials to England in exchange for goods and did little trading in other parts, soon ran up a staggering deficit in London. Farming or speculating in land, selling rum to the West Indies, supplying ship stores and building ships, fishing and whaling, these were the favoured businesses of colonial Americans. As these were mainly dealings in raw and strategic materials, they suited the sea-borne and industrial British very well. The American colonies were admirable in their supply of primary materials and consumption of goods that docked first in London. Ominously, however, the Yankees were a resourceful and inventive people, as their home and village industries showed.

The self-sufficiency of the American farm was proverbial and gave rise to a whole way of thought, which still opposes welfare and considers that people should save and store enough to tide them over hard winters. Nearly all necessities were made on the farm itself, which adopted not only European methods, but also the sophisticated vegetables and techniques of local Indian tribes. And it was the Indian potato which, in a sense, helped to dispossess the Indian, for when the crop failed in Ireland, the peasants were forced to emigrate to its original home.

There was a rough division of labour between the sexes on the farm, rather like the division between the colonies and the mother country. The men produced and brought in raw materials from the cleared earth and the forest, the woman processed these materials for use. Few women, other than Indians and slaves and German immigrants, worked in the fields, except at harvest-time. Their province was the house and sometimes the orchard and farmyard. The fit men gathered the grain, the timber, and the meat, while women and children and old men made the farmhouse into a little factory, preparing and preserving food, spinning and sewing, washing and ironing and mending clothes, making candles and soap.

A wife was necessary for every farmer, and colonial America was largely agricultural. 'In a wild country where it is almost impossible to hire assistance of any kind either male or female,' a traveller in the backwoods wrote, 'a man is thrown entirely upon his resources.' These resources or lack of them usually made him into a hunter or trapper, for a farmer could not manage alone. The very size of the vacant land and shortage of labour made

After the hunter and trapper came the farmer. Log cabins, like the small one shown on the right, were introduced into America by Scandinavian settlers.

This prosperous farm belonged to Edward Hicks's Quaker foster-father, David Twining.

Americans elevate hard work for everyone into the chief virtue, if not the sole reason, of life. The savings from this work allowed more expansion and clearing of the soil or else provided for the inevitable bad times and barren seasons of the farmer. 'The tenants of his house, like the beasts of his farm,' Crèvecoeur wrote in his famous *Letters from an American Farmer*, 'must now depend on the collected stores of the preceding season, sagaciously distributed and prepared by the industry of his wife. There lies the *aurum potabile* of an American farmer. He may work and gather the choicest fruits of his farm; but if female economy fails, he loses the comfort of good victuals.'

Thus marriage and children and family life were the usual choices of American society. Girls were encouraged to wed young; a single woman was rare. If she was strong, and even if she was an ugly widow with many children, she had difficulty not in finding a husband, but in refusing one.

Arx Carolina, the old fortified settlement between the rivers Ashley and Cooper at Charleston, South Carolina.

Wives were honoured, while old maids were not. And to bring children to a second husband was an advantage, for each child meant another pair of hands, while food for their keep was cheap and abundant.

Where everybody toiled, few could complain about the injustice of labour everlasting – except on Sundays in religious households. Some farmers treated their wives as little more than beasts of burden: one Western American settler was quoted as saying: 'I reckon women are some like horses and oxen, the biggest can do the most work, and that's what I want one for.' Yet most men treated their wives and dependent female relatives with some respect, even though a wife did not even exist separate from her husband in the eyes of the patriarchal English law.

The taming of the wilderness meant equality in slavery to the earth; only after clearing and planting and building could there be talk of equality between colonies and mother country, between slave and free, and, in the millennium, between men and women. When there was an urban and town society with some intervals of leisure, talk of rebellion, first against England, then against slavery and the saloon and male domination, became heard.

Before that time of small relief from toil, protest could only be tiny, as in the hint of rebellion in the works of America's first poet, Anne Bradstreet:

It is but vain unjustly to wage war,
Men can do best, and women know it well.
Pre-eminence in all and each is yours –
Yet grant some small acknowledgement of ours.

As early as the eighteenth century, urban and town society had become important in America. The cities of Philadelphia, New York, Boston, Charlestown, and Newport had tens of thousands of inhabitants. They faced towards Europe and imported new ideas. Crèvecoeur's description of New York at the time of the Revolution tells of a handsome city of 28,000 people, flourishing on trade because of its vital position as the hinge on the lower route between Europe and the American interior. 'Nothing is more beautiful,' he wrote, 'and nothing gives the reflective spectator a higher idea of the city's wealth, or of the nature of its free and happy commerce, than the multitude of ships of all sizes, which continually tack about in the bay.'

Forty years later Charleston had grown almost beyond recognition. Its busy docks handled a succession of specialized goods: rice, indigo, tobacco, timber and cotton.

Contemporary comment.

With the tolerance and competition of city life, traditional ideas often gave away before speculative or rebellious notions. The contagion of innovation spread out to some of the small towns that clustered about their founding city, particularly about Boston – and no American city was then much more than a glorified town. Only the filthy and corrupt vast cities of Europe horrified the American mind; no one wanted the great wen of London or Pope-ridden Rome to cross the Atlantic with their slums, grime, and starving rabble. Such cities were to Crèvecoeur 'the confined theatre of cupidity', while the New World represented limitless opportunity.

The expanding cities and towns of North America with their concentration of labour provided opportunity for manufacturers. In this enterprise, however, the colonists came up against their inferior status. They were British subjects; thus they were subject to Britain's commercial laws, which wanted to keep colonies as underdeveloped countries tied to the British market. Manufacturers' lobbies in London put pressure on the Board of Trade to suppress competition. 'A colonist cannot make a button, a horse-shoe, nor a hobnail,' a Boston newspaper cried in 1765, 'but some sooty iron-monger or respectable buttonmaker of Britain shall bawl and squall that his honour's worship is most egregiously maltreated, injured, cheated, and robbed by the rascally American Republicans.' American traders overseas were not naturally republicans; no one liked better the protection of the King's navy against pirates. Yet navigation laws made them republicans despite themselves.

Other annoyances provoked the colonists into a revolt. It was not the slack government of George III's ministers and agents that led to the Declaration of Independence so much as their firm government. Restrictive laws on the books hurt nobody; in practice, they foment riots. The Sugar Act of 1764 and the Stamp Act of 1765 were intended to raise revenue from the foreign sugar trade and from legal documents, to help to pay for the English war debt and the expanded defence system in the Americas. The enforcement of these Acts led to vigorous opposition and their swift withdrawal, although the British government still declared its right to tax the colonies from Westminster. The Townshend Acts of 1767 put duties on many consumer goods in the Atlantic colonies, and, what was worse, provided for an efficient customs service to collect the taxes. Many Americans on the coast were fishermen or smugglers at heart, just as in the interior they were farmers or hunters; few thought it right to pay taxes on what they

Two stamps.

imported or took directly from land or sea. The colonists reacted to these measures with a boycott of British goods, which halved English imports and led to the partial repeal of the hated Acts.

Now Asia intervened to worsen the situation. Due to mismanagement, the East India Company was failing. So the British government granted it a monopoly of importing tea into the New World (George III's ministers might have remembered that it was opposition to monopolies granted by the Crown which had contributed to Parliament's revolt in England in the seventeenth century). Boston's reaction to the monopoly was a Tea Party in which citizens disguised as Indians dumped a whole cargo of tea into the harbour. Retaliation bred retaliation. The British reply was the 'Intolerable Acts', which closed Boston harbour until an indemnity was paid, revised the Charter of Massachusetts, provided for trial in England for capital offenders, and insisted on the quartering of troops on the local population. Furthermore, the territory between the Ohio Valley and the Great Lakes was annexed to the province of Quebec, thus preventing the westward expansion of the Atlantic colonies, which thought the hinterlands were theirs by right.

Boston Tea Party

The Stamp Act became the focus of American grievances. Even though it was swiftly withdrawn (the English satire below refers to this), the bitterness remained – only to be further reinforced by the Townshend Acts of 1767.

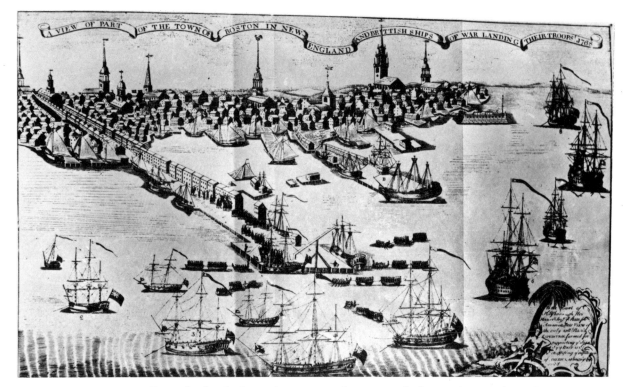

Troops landing in Boston in 1768, to enforce unpopular laws and to guard British interests. This was one of Paul Revere's most important engravings.

A greater boycott of English goods followed and provoked a slump in England. British counter-measures involved an embargo on trade with New England and the exclusion of Yankee fishermen from the teeming Grand Banks of Newfoundland. The slump spread to America and led to dis-affection and rioting. The economy of the Atlantic colonies had left behind the barter and agricultural stage, and had begun on its cycle of booms and slumps that were to become as expected as the phases of the moon.

The colonists were used to riots. Frequently the authority of the King's governor had been challenged by a group of debtor farmers, who had picked up their rifles rather than pay their creditors. The remoteness of government had led to the independence of the frontiersmen, and the cry of 'No taxation without representation' seemed to add justice to the side of those who merely wished for no taxation at all. The independent American government after the Revolution was to find it just as difficult to collect taxes and was to be faced with the same backwoods rebellions. Yet, for the moment, even sophisticated Americans thought it reasonable that the British army in the

'The Bloody Massacre'. This engraving by Paul Revere was almost pure propaganda, as can be seen from the 'Butchers Hall' sign above the custom house. Far from commanding a firing squad, Captain Prescott risked his life to try and prevent bloodshed.

Victims of the 'Boston Massacre'.

New World should be subsidized solely by taxes on British merchants, who made large profits on trade with the American colonies.

A successful revolution demands hatred of an enemy, love of a distinct group or place or faith, and organizers of genius. The American Revolution had all three elements. England was hated for its remoteness and its pretensions of control: by 1775 only a minority of Americans had ever seen the mother country and, as Thomas Paine pointed out, there was 'something absurd in supposing a Continent to be perpetually governed by an island'. Fear of the centralized Anglican Church trying to expand in the New World led to religious hate, fear of heavy taxation and business controls passed by an absentee Parliament led to economic hate, fear of British intentions to block westward expansion and independent action led to political hate.

Love of land and town and city and North America was already rooted in the colonies; in the first intercolonial congress of 1765 against the Stamp Act, a deputy from South Carolina declared: 'There ought to be no New England man, no New Yorker, known on the continent, but all of us

Patrick Henry.

Samuel Adams.

Americans.' The sentiment of difference from Europe, dramatized by the long memory of the Atlantic crossing and of flight from oppression, made many of the colonists see themselves as Americans. They felt that they belonged to where they were; some had families that had settled generations ago and found the New World already old. It was among these most passionate of Americans that the coming revolution discovered its organizers of genius: men such as Sam Adams, Thomas Jefferson, and Patrick Henry, who with their 'committees of correspondence' set up a network of resistance, called meetings of local leaders, and saw to the boycott of British goods.

Thus the 2,500,000 free colonists of North America, already one-third as many as the population of England, veered towards revolution. Distance had bred a tradition of alienation. The wilderness had insensibly adapted imported European institutions to meet its own demands. The New World had taken in the immigrants of the Old; but its newness had changed them into a new people, Americans rather than Europeans at one remove. With the King more than three thousand miles away, a local government elected by the votes of white male property-holders – and outside of the South, most white male Americans were property-holders – was the visible fact.

If, in John Adams's opinion, one-third of the colonists remained loyal to England, it was because the wilderness made people of conservative tempera-ment cling even harder to their traditions and because the wealthy feared to lose everything by a revolution, which might turn out to be social as well as political. Moreover, British sea power had a deterrent effect on the coastal cities facing towards Europe; few settled families thought that the mighty British Empire could lose the war. Thus the coming of the revolution caused ugly splits in American society, between the merchant and the frontiersman, between the port city and the back country, between the planter dependent on the London market and the small farmer who hated taxes and tight credit.

Despite the leadership of such rich Virginia planters as George Washing-ton, the rebel colonists were, on the whole, 'the plain people, as distinguished from the aristocracy'. The Tories, who stood by the British, were mostly those with power and property to lose. In the succeeding war the Tories were to lose all they had; many of them fled to Canada, where they set up a more enduring part of the British Empire and baulked the victorious Americans from taking over the whole of the northern part of the continent, the logical conclusion of American independence.

As for the Indians, they were now doomed to lose their lands even faster. 'The ruin of these tribes', de Tocqueville observed in 1831, 'began from the day when Europeans landed on their shores; it has proceeded ever since. . . . They seem to have been placed by Providence amid the riches of the New World only to enjoy them for a season; they were there merely to wait till others came.' They had either to join the new Americans, which was nearly impossible, or be evicted and eliminated by them. The Declaration of Independence accused George III of bringing on to the frontier settlements 'the merciless Indian savages, whose known rule of warfare is an un- distinguished destruction of all ages, sexes and conditions'. The colonists applied the same rule of warfare to the Indians; the toast drunk by the rebel general sent to harry the Iroquois, the old allies of the British, was: 'Civiliza- tion or death to all American savages.' It was too late for half-measures; a continent could be won. As Robert Frost commented later from the full security of being an American first and foremost:

> The land was ours before we were the land's.
> She was our land more than a hundred years
> Before we were her people. She was ours
> In Massachusetts, in Virginia,
> But we were England's, still colonials . . .
> Such as we were we gave ourselves outright
> (The deed of gift was many deeds of war)
> To the land vaguely realizing westward . . .

Indians. A detail from an engraving in John Smith's *Discovery of Virginia*, 1609.

The Declaration of Independence, 4 July 1776.

Chapter Two

THE AMERICAN REVOLUTION
AND THE VIRGINIA DYNASTY

When Thomas Jefferson drafted the Declaration of Independence in 1776, *Declaration of* he used 'what had been hackneyed in Congress for two years before'. The *Independence* famous document, which sought to justify the rebellion, was remarkable for its lack of revolutionary fire. It represented the legalism of the American rebel leaders, their hatred of a liberty which could be called anarchy. They wanted to distinguish themselves as clearly from the savages in the wilderness as from the tyrannies of Europe.

They based their case for rebellion on the need of men for a government deriving its 'just powers from the consent of the governed'; they were far from glorifying the right of the individual to rebel. The people *as a whole* were declared to have the right to alter or abolish a tyrannical government; a single rebel had no right of revolt. The Declaration of Independence was a declaration of the independence of the American colonies from the tyranny of one man, George III. Its price was to insist on the conformity of the individual American to the sovereignty of the people.

Two days before the Declaration of Independence was adopted by the representatives of the rebellious states at the Second Continental Congress, a resolution by a Virginian, Richard Henry Lee, was passed that 'these United Colonies are, and of right ought to be, Free and Independent States.' The resolution merely confirmed local initiative and resistance. In Massachu-setts the colonials had already fought at Bunker Hill and were up in arms all over New England. The prestige and wealth of the Virginia planters made the Congress choose one of them, George Washington, as commander-in-chief of the colonial forces. Yet, in spite of his attempts to form and keep

CHARLES TOWN

BOSTON

The Battle of Bunker Hill, 17 June 1775. A demoralizing tactical disaster for the British.

together a Continental Army through harvests and winters, most of the American resistance was local defence or assault against the Tories and redcoats.

British strategy for the war was based on the French strategy against the thirteen colonies, while the colonists adopted old British tactics. The Americans tried to capture Canada to break through British encirclement; they were repulsed, only to capture the whole of Burgoyne's army when he tried to counter-attack down the Hudson. On their side, the British remembered the Dutch threat at New Amsterdam and split the northern from the southern colonies by occupying New York and Philadelphia. They hoped that the states, already bickering among themselves, would splinter apart naturally and merely need brushing up.

Moreover, the British used the French device of inciting Indian tribes to harass the frontiers of the states; this policy kept many reinforcements from Washington on guard duty at their homes. Only the intervention of the

Congress voted independence in July 1776 (*above*), and fourteen months later America won its first major victory at Saratoga (*below*), where Burgoyne, general and playwright, surrendered to Gates.

Spanish and the French on the side of the colonists made the British finally lose a losing war, for they could hardly hope to overcome the colonists' first line of defence, the great moat of the Atlantic. The brief French control of Virginia waters led to the surrender of Cornwallis with the last large British army at Yorktown in 1781. Sea power was the one necessity for keeping a grip on the American continent.

The peace treaty that followed recognized the independence of the American states. Their confines were to stretch south from the Great Lakes and east from the Mississippi. Britain still thought of encirclement and retained its rights on West Florida, but this thorn in the southern flank of the Americans was soon restored to Spain. Proposals for free trade between Britain and its ex-colonies came to nothing because of mutual suspicion, while the new republic looked uneasily at its allies, monarchist France and Spain, and wondered how to scotch their designs and take over their possessions in the New World.

The surrender of Lord Cornwallis. Lord Cornwallis himself was ill and his deputy, General O'Hara, surrendered to Washington's deputy, General Lincoln. Painting by John Trumbull, Yale University Art Gallery.

The
Washington
family by
Edward Savage,
1796.

George Washington, unexpectedly, did not try to become the ruler of the *George*
new country. He was truly a republican, despite Horace Walpole's worldly *Washington*
belief that 'the American leaders will not easily part with dictatorships and
consulships to retire to their private ploughs.' Washington behaved exactly
like an early Roman, returning to the life of a Virginia planter. Perhaps he
was waiting for a recall to power because of the weak government resulting
from the ineffective Articles of Confederation among the American states.
More likely, he was a man of both conviction and realism, who knew that
King George of Mount Vernon would be resisted as fiercely as King George
of Windsor Castle.

The new nation was not a mass democracy. There were no more than
400,000 free adult men in the whole of the United States, perhaps one in
seven of the population. The rest were disenfranchised or enslaved, Indians,
Negroes, women, bond-servants, children, aliens, and the insane. In this
privileged male caste, fewer than one in three were allowed to vote, and, in
the South, voters only went to the polls to support the local planters. Society
outside the backwoods and the turbulent Atlantic cities was controlled
largely by the wealthy and the aristocratic.

These men looked on the early years of the republic with fear. City mobs threatened property, debtor farmers rose in open revolt in Shays's Rebellion. The Articles of Confederation did not work. Congress could not collect its taxes, raise a standing army, honour its debts, or regulate trade either internally or abroad. Local interest in the states effectively managed policy and taxation without any reference to the national interest. Speculators squabbled over western lands, while the splinter communities of Vermont and Kentucky clamoured vainly for recognition under the Northwest Ordinance of 1787, which allowed for the creation of new states in the West. In this creeping chaos, men of substance decided to review the federal system and write a constitution, which would replace the hopes of the Declaration of Independence with a government of 'checks and balances' suited to gentlemen of independent means. Representatives of the states met at a convention in Philadelphia in 1787 to draw up this constitution.

Nothing shows better the importance of property to the Founding Fathers than their equation of ownership with joy. Jefferson had defined the chief rights of men as 'life, liberty and the pursuit of happiness'; the Founding Fathers defined them as 'life, liberty and property'. Deliberately, the revolutionary hope that a man might seek for whatever satisfactions he wanted in life was changed to the conservative law that a man's things were his own by right. The ideal of being was changed into the fact of holding or getting, for the Founding Fathers presumed that life and liberty meant freedom for other Americans to try and become as rich and powerful as they were, not to reject riches and power for the chimera of equality among men. Such equality of property they equated with a mean levelling, which would drag down the good rather than elevate the bad. De Tocqueville later confirmed their judgement when he reported that he had never found a country 'where the love of money has taken stronger hold on the affections of men and where a profounder contempt is expressed for the theory of the permanent equality of property'.

The American Constitution The Constitution was written by men of property for men of property; but it was also written to make a strong nation out of the bickering states. Two legislatures were set up, the House of Representatives elected directly on the basis of population every two years, and the Senate elected indirectly on the basis of two Senators from each state serving six years at a time. The small states now felt protected by the Senate from being swallowed up by the large popular vote of the big states. The South demanded two further compromises

Gladstone described the American Constitution, which was signed on 17 September 1787, as 'the most wonderful work ever struck off at a given time by the brain and purpose of man'.

to preserve its position against the North. In calculating the liability of each state for direct taxes and membership of the House of Representatives, a slave was to be counted as three-fifths of a free man (his missing two-fifths presumably included his love of citizenship and liberty), while taxes on exports were forbidden for ever and interference with the slave trade blocked for twenty years. Moreover, a clause that two-thirds of the Senate had to approve of all treaties with foreign powers gave a minority bloc in the Senate the power to veto foreign policy.

The executive power was put in the hands of a President, to be chosen every four years by an Electoral College, itself picked by the legislatures or the people of the states. The President had the right to enforce laws, appoint a Cabinet and judges, make treaties, and command the army and navy. A Supreme Court was also created; its nine Justices had life tenure and were the final court of appeal in law; its duties included the interpretation of the Constitution and federal law. Furthermore, the value of the dollar was protected by forbidding the states to pay their debts in anything but silver or gold or to pass laws letting debtors off their debts. The states were protected by keeping residual rights not expressly given to the federal government, yet the federal government was free to expand its powers by using them and setting up precedents.

Washington (*opposite*) thought the Constitution a hopeful experiment; Madison (*above left*), President after Jefferson, was pleased with it, and Hamilton (*above right*) regarded it as an imperfect compromise.

The Constitution was brief and unclear; it allowed room for development. Although it was built, in the words of one of its chief architects, James Madison, 'for the ages', it could be amended. A Bill of Rights in ten amendments was, indeed, promised to settle the fears of individuals that the federal government might attack their rights.

The Constitution was not ratified easily by the states. It had not been written, as Washington himself demanded, simply to 'please the people'; Alexander Hamilton, the brilliant soldier and financier from New York, wanted it to 'check the imprudence of democracy'. Just as Cromwell had had to crush the Levellers to prove that the Commonwealth in England had not brought about a social revolution, so the Founding Fathers had to curb such demagogues as Patrick Henry by writing a constitution which would prove the American Revolution to be merely political.

The Constitution was eventually ratified, because it promised a better government than the preceding one. No state or interest felt that it could not influence or delay some branch of the government. As Madison complained during the Convention, there was too much thought about 'the necessity of opposing one vice and interest to another vice and interest'. Yet the checks and balances written into the Constitution allowed everyone to feel that he could defend his liberties by constitutional means. Revolution was no longer necessary to provide for freedom under the law; the Constitution even allowed its own change.

President Washington　　Washington was elected unopposed to the Presidency, soothing the fears of Virginia about the new form of government. He defined many of the powers of his office. 'I walk on untrodden ground', he wrote. 'There is scarcely any part of my conduct which may not hereafter be drawn into precedent.' He walked firmly, yet circumspectly; but he definitely made the President the first man in the nation. The new capital of the United States

Two New York landmarks: Federal Hall (*above*) and the Tontine Coffee House (*left*), the nerve centre of the city's commerce.

was named after him and was slowly built on the borders of his home state. He also founded a dynasty of Virginia planter Presidents, who were to occupy the office for eight terms out of the first nine. Virginia, the mother of the American colonies, was also the mother of the first Presidents. It was ironical that the power of the Presidency would be used to crush rebellious Virginia in the Civil War.

Two of Washington's appointments were vital. Hamilton, a great admirer of Julius Caesar and of the constitutional monarchy of England, became Secretary of the Treasury: he immediately provided for the funding of the public debt and for financing the government through customs and excise taxes and the founding of the First Bank of the United States. Appointments to the customs houses, incidentally, gave the government its first powers of patronage and led to the spoils system, by which the gainers of power can reward their friends and punish their enemies by giving or taking away their official jobs.

Secondly, Washington appointed his Virginia neighbour, Thomas Jefferson, to be Secretary of State; Jefferson was the compleat gentleman of the eighteenth century, planter, scholar, inventor, expert or dabbler in every art and science. Despite a sympathy for the French Revolution, he kept the new nation from joining in the wars that again engulfed the Old World, where traditional governments were bent on crushing the new republic of France. It was Jefferson who warned against 'entangling alliances' with Europe – a phrase which came to roost on George Washington.

When Washington insisted on retiring at the end of eight years, thus creating a precedent that two terms should be enough for any President, he had reason to feel pleased in his 'Farewell Address', drafted by the ambitious Hamilton. The Constitution had been made to work; the United States was accepted as a strong power. Despite provocation by British and French seizure of American trading vessels, the United States was still at peace. Although he did not mention it, Washington could also take pride in the Bill of Rights, which protected constitutionally the religion and rights of the individual, including his rights to free speech, reasonable bail, speedy trial, and the possession of firearms to resist an intolerable government. Yet Washington felt disquiet at what proved to be the most enduring legacy of his administration, the growth of underground political parties. 'All Parties', as Cobbett rightly observed, 'affected to regret the loss of Washington, but none were truly Sorry.' For with his going, the divisions of the politicians could show themselves.

Political Parties
Hamilton and his friends supported England and opposed the French Revolution; they tried to push Washington into declaring war out of an obsessive fear that unruly mobs with French ideas of equality would bring a social revolution to the New World. They called themselves Federalists and wanted a strong centralized power. Against them stood Jefferson and the first Republicans, who supported the early stages of the French Revolution and stood for States' Rights and the farmers against federal authority.

Although Kentucky and Vermont had been admitted into the Union, the Westerners felt that the government did not protect them enough against Indians, incited by the British and the Spanish to prevent the westward migration of American settlers. They also felt that the Hamiltonians were interested only in trade and industry and good relations with England; they were particularly bitter over the Jay Treaty, which may have made the British leave a few frontier forts, but which recognized British claims in midwestern

John Jay.

John Adams and his wife, Abigail, whose opinions on women's rights were considerably ahead of her time.

areas already settled by American families. Taking advantage of this dis-content, Jefferson and Madison formed an alliance between disgruntled Southern planters and Western farmers and even brought in a new political organization in New York City, the Sons of St Tammany which the manipulating Aaron Burr had created against Hamilton on his home ground. These new committees of correspondence cultivated grass-roots support against the Federalists and the manufacturing interests of New England.

John Adams

The Federalists held on to the Presidency in 1796; their candidate, John Adams from Massachusetts, just beat Jefferson, who became Vice President. Adams was a sound political theorist, but unfit, in Hamilton's opinion, for 'the *administration* of government'. He remained surrounded by inferior Federalists and could not escape the shadow of the retired Washington. He complained that he was not really President in his own right, but only viceroy under Washington while Washington was viceroy under Hamilton. Hamilton, now operating outside the government, did keep his influence over the retired President; 'he was an *Aegis*', he confessed on Washington's death in 1799, '*very essential to me*'. This death of the father-figure of the republic was too late to allow Adams to be President on his own; it also buried in the grave the ambitions of the restless and feared Hamilton.

America's running skirmish with the French and the English continued till the Treaty of Ghent in 1815. Here an American privateer is being captured by the English.

John Marshall.

Adams had difficulty in keeping out of war with France, which treated America's envoys with disdain. The French seized numerous American ships on the pretext that they were trading with Britain; the Americans retaliated by privateering against the French. Because of spying activities by the European powers, the Federalists in Congress pushed through Alien and Sedition Acts giving the President power to expel foreigners and proceed against Americans who defamed the government. Adams was unwise to allow the Sedition Act to be used against the Republican Press; as a Federalist journal declared: 'It is patriotism to write in favour of our government – it is sedition to write against it.' The Republicans replied with the Virginia and Kentucky Resolutions, which defended States' Rights against federal power and laid the ground for the later secession of the South. Jefferson even declared that the legsilature of each state had the right to declare unconstitutional 'within its own territory' federal laws which it disliked.

With these cracks showing in the structure of the new Union, the election of 1800 was held. Luckily, Jefferson and Burr won a majority in the Electoral College and Jefferson became President. As a last delaying action, Adams packed the new circuit and district courts with Federalist judges and put in as Chief Justice of the Supreme Court, a Federalist, John Marshall, whose 'twistifications' would 'reconcile law to his personal biases'.

Thomas Jefferson by Rembrandt Peale. ▶

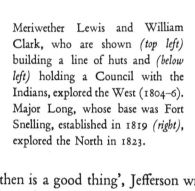

Meriwether Lewis and William Clark, who are shown *(top left)* building a line of huts and *(below left)* holding a Council with the Indians, explored the West (1804–6). Major Long, whose base was Fort Snelling, established in 1819 *(right)*, explored the North in 1823.

Thomas Jefferson 'A little rebellion now and then is a good thing', Jefferson wrote before he was President; but once in office he became the apostle of federal power and national unity. Although he supported an uncensored Press and grants of free land for Western schools, he wanted American democracy to be led by a strong government which could expand the nation's frontiers. He did not believe in the people enough to increase the limited suffrage or to stop large-scale speculation in land. If once he had declared, 'Let our workshops remain in Europe', for fear that urban mobs would corrupt agrarian democracy, as President he gave American industry the whole home market by forbidding the import of British goods. He did nothing to undo Hamilton's strong system of government finance, although he did reduce federal expenditure enough to get rid of the hated whisky tax and lower the national debt. Even Hamilton's death in a duel at the hands of Burr did not end his political influence although Burr's career was now buried except for certain machinations that verged on treason.

In fact, Jefferson was like Washington, a man who tried to give something to everyone. His first statement in office was a healing one: 'We are all

republicans – we are all federalists.' These precedents in American policy were to continue without a break, until the Federalists complained that the Republicans had 'out-Federalized Federalism'.

Yet Jefferson brought about one revolution in favour of the farmers and land speculation, which would upset the structure of American politics. He called the West into existence to redress the balance between North and South. He sent out Lewis and Clark to explore the unknown hinterlands as far as Oregon and kept his eyes turned towards the Mississippi rather than the Atlantic. Nothing could persuade him to go to war with Britain or France, despite endless humiliations inflicted on American ships; he was prepared to ruin the American carrying trade and risk the secession of New England during the fourteen months of his Embargo Act, which bottled up American ships in home ports so that they would avoid British provocations. In fact, Jefferson was unwittingly founding a policy of economic nationalism and isolation, the 'American System', which was to develop the United Stares for a century by turning its energies inwards on its western lands rather than oveseas to distant colonies and conflict with Europe.

His patience had its reasons. For each inch he lost on the seas, he gained a league in the American wilderness. He agreed with the scoffing Virginia leader of Congress, John Randolph: 'What, shall this great mammoth of the American forest leave her native element and plunge into the water in a mad contest with the shark? . . . why take to the waters where you can neither fight nor swim?' While the British navy kept the rest of Europe out of the New World, Jefferson worked at breaking out of the Spanish encirclement of the southern states.

The Louisiana Purchase Napoleon, whose grandiose vision included the conquest of the New World, had annexed all the Spanish territory called Louisiana between the Mississippi River and the Rockies. But the French armies trying to reconquer the sugar plantations of Haiti were decimated by disease and rebellious slaves, who made Haiti the second free republic in the hemisphere. Moreover, the British navy prevented any large French invasion of the Caribbean. So Napoleon sold the whole Louisiana territory to Jefferson for a mere $15,000,000, the best property deal ever made since Adam and Eve were given the title to the earth. Napoleon was fearful, indeed, that the British might overrun Louisiana, let alone the American frontiersmen; he would rather New Orleans went to Britain's enemies than to Britain. As French colonies could not exist in the New World without sea power, it was better to sell than fight; Jefferson had already warned, the possessor of New Orleans was America's 'natural and habitual enemy'.

By 1796 the Mohawk River had been made navigable for small boats as far inland as Rome. This in turn encouraged further westward expansion.

New Orleans in 1841, looking from the middle of Picayune Ferry. An aquatint by W. Bennett, Mabel Brady Garvan Collection, Yale University Art Gallery.

This vast acquisition of American land upset the scale of American politics. Jefferson had opened up the way for his vaunted republic of small farmers; agrarian democracy could prosper in the new West. Since the War of Independence the settlers had been moving westward over the Appalachians, along the trails blazed by the trappers and frontiersmen. Some had crossed the mountains of Pennsylvania or had passed through the Cumberland Gap behind Daniel Boone until they reached the tributaries of the Mississippi and could build rafts or flatboats to float farther towards the sunset. Some moved up into the plateaus of the Appalachians and remained in the new states of Kentucky and Tennessee; forgotten by the mainstreams of westward migration, these mountain people preserved the folk-ways of the eighteenth century for the sociologists of the twentieth.

Ohio was made safe for settlement after the Indians had been defeated there in 1794; nine years later, it was admitted as a state into the Union. The frontier was pushed onwards to Indiana and Illinois. The westering Yankees

A house in the French Quarter, built c. 1850.

St Louis in 1836. After the Louisiana Purchase of 1803, St Louis became a gateway to the West, and with the immigrants came new industries to compete with the fur trade.

here mingled with the westering Virginians, while down in the Southwest the Southerners pushed forward the frontier of the cotton kingdom against Indian resistance. After all, Acts of Congress allowed the purchase of small parcels of western land from the government at a mere half-dollar an acre, and the soil of the Atlantic states was already growing poorer from too much cultivation.

Yet even this feast of virgin land did not satisfy the Westerners; they wanted an orgy of soil and speculation. They joined the Southern planters in a group called the 'War Hawks', to put pressure on Jefferson to fight Spain for the Floridas, and Britain for Canada. But Jefferson would not do so, even though he predicted that the rapid growth of the American population would 'cover the whole northern, if not the southern continent'. The United States had just doubled its size; it had to digest before it could swallow more.

Jefferson left his office of 'splendid misery' to his neighbour and adviser, James Madison, a man of much political learning and little stature;

Washington Irving called him 'but a withered little applejohn'. He may have been the theorist and father of the Constitution, but he nearly proved to be the undertaker of the Union. Although he continued the Hamiltonian system of finance by founding a Second Bank of the United States once the charter of the First had been allowed to lapse, and although he tried to be as strong a President as Jefferson in his use of federal power, he went to war wrongly and he fought it badly and by his errors he prejudiced his country.

A new breed of frontier politician came to Congress in 1810. The leadership in the House soon fell to Henry Clay, a brilliant orator from Kentucky, ably backed by John C. Calhoun from the southern frontier of South Carolina. An Indian war had begun in the North; the tribe of the great Shawnee, Tecumseh, had been massacred by the troops of the Governor of Indiana Territory, William Henry Harrison, at Tippecanoe in 1811. Tecumseh had counter-attacked, and the British were accused of inciting him when he needed no incitement. On the high seas British press-gangs continued to seize American sailors off their ships. Madison bowed to pressure and asked Congress to declare a second War of Independence against Britain in 1812; the prize this time was the whole North American continent and the freedom of the seas.

The Battle of Tippecanoe, 1811. Expansion was at the cost of the Indian, and resistance merely accelerated the process.

The Battle of Borgne Bay, 14 December 1814. The British defeated the American flotilla that attempted to stop their landing below New Orleans.

The war itself clipped the wings of the War Hawks. After Perry's victory on the waters of Lake Erie, an attempted invasion of Canada ended in the burning of the parliament houses of Toronto and in quick retreat. The British retaliated by burning the White House and the Capitol in 1814, while Madison and Congress fled pitiably from Washington to the back country. The huge distances over which the war was fought still made any victory unlikely; neither side could effectively occupy the territory of the other. Strategy, however, remained constant, the war of the great land mammoth against the shark. The Americans tried to crush Canada, while the British bit at the American ports and New Orleans in an attempt to carry out the old plan of confining the Americans east of the Mississippi River.

Significantly, the first terms that the British demanded from the American peace commissioners resurrected the royal proclamation of 1763 and demanded an Indian buffer state on the Great Lakes and Canadian access to the upper reaches of the Mississippi. The final peace treaty was signed at Ghent, without any great change in the position of either side, except that Britain withdrew most of its claims to the Midwest. Three weeks after the treaty was signed, the Kentucky general, Andrew Jackson, won a short, bloody, and unnecessary battle against the best of the British army at New Orleans. His victory rubbed in the fact that the western plains and their watery gate had gone to the United States for ever.

On 8 January, Andrew Jackson (*left*) defeated the British at the Battle of New Orleans (*above*). Ironically, the Treaty of Ghent had already been signed in Holland fifteen days before, but the document did not reach America until 11 February.

Some Indians were immediately assimilated (*far left*), but most attempted to preserve their way of life. Unfortunately, westward expansion paid no heed to territorial agreements, and when the Indians justifiably rebelled (*centre left*), the

The peace came just in time to preserve the young republic. The states of New England were near secession; their trade had been ruined first by the Embargo Act and now by the failure of the Atlantic war, except for privateering against British merchantmen. The General Court of Massachusetts reported in 1814 that Madison had deserted the principles of States' Rights, which he had upheld in *The Federalist* and in the Virginia and Kentucky Resolutions. 'Whenever the national compact is violated and the citizens of this State are oppressed by cruel and unauthorized laws,' the report declared, 'the Legislature is bound to interpose its power and wrest from the oppressor his victim. This is the spirit of our Union', and this was the spirit that Madison had once praised and now denied.

A convention was called at Hartford by the Federalists of three New England states to bring about secession; but the end of the war made the convention ridiculous and tainted the Federalists with the show of treason. Madison had provoked the crisis by his original doctrine of States' Rights and by his acceptance of a stupid war that seemed to promise only bankruptcy to the trading North. The Virginia dynasty seemed to New England to be ruling in the sectional interests of South and West alone.

The War of 1812 had, however, led to the suppression of the Indians in the Southwest by Andrew Jackson. The policy of the removal of whole Indian tribes was begun; the original inhabitants of the eastern parts of the

white man sought vengeance (*centre right*), and destroyed proud men like Geronimo (*below right*) of whom today's Indian (*far right*) is but a lustreless reflection.

United States were deported beyond the Mississippi. Even those tribes which, like the Cherokees in Georgia, were reasonably civilized and won court decisions in their favour were driven off their lands. These displaced Indians had to fight the Indians of the Great Plains to survive on their new locations on the edge of the frontier. Thus Indian slaughtered Indian, because of the pressure of the pioneers behind him.

The pioneers moved on fearlessly and remorselessly. Their tools were the rifle and the axe. They performed prodigies of clearing in the great forests of the Midwest, which stretched as far as the ninety-eighth meridian. Wild life was decimated, the timber chopped down; for the wood was needed to build cabins, boardwalks, schools, churches, fences, river landing-stages, and eventually to make sleepers for railroads. Once the land had been cleared, the plough turned over the virgin soil, and wagons and flatboats took the crops across the mountains or down the Mississippi to New Orleans. In the wake of the pioneer men came horses and oxen and women, until each clearing supported a farm family, with sparse small towns scattered about to provide a few goods and a little education and religion. Even more rarely in the new West, a larger town grew up on a river junction or an important trail, such as Pittsburgh, Cincinnati, or St Louis. These embryo cities were the hubs of civilization, with the small towns spoking out on the surrounding trails and passing on the influences of urban life to the neighbouring farms.

Westering

Though the country was opened up by the trapper (*right*), he was swiftly followed by the settler (*above*) who combined farming with trapping and hunting.

A form of 'Western fever' drove the pioneers to quit their safe farms in the East: an urge for better and cheaper land, a wish for independence and self-assertion, an idea that it might still be possible to find Eden as well as El Dorado in the Mississippi Valley. So they left the security of the Atlantic states – sometimes the populations of whole villages at a time – for the speculative benefits and certain rigours of the West. Men and women would walk for some thousand miles, if they were too poor to buy horses. Disease, loneliness and want were not enough to deter the restlessness of pioneer families who moved ever westward after a few years on the edge of the frontier, as though paradise on earth really existed just over the next river or range.

But these first Westerners were pioneers of the forest. When they reached the ninety-eighth meridian, just beyond the Mississippi, they saw the Great Plains rolling ahead of them like the sea all the way to the foot of the Rocky Mountains. The sight of such a treeless and largely waterless waste persuaded the first pioneers that a Great American Desert lay in front of them. As Francis Parkman described the Nebraska scene: 'the level monotony of the plain was unbroken as far as the eye could reach. Sometimes it glared in the

As the pioneers moved west, solitary cabins soon become settlements such as this one in the Northwest, *c.* 1860 (*above*). But those who hunted animals for their living (*left*), often did not welcome the advance of civilization.

sun, an expanse of hot, bare sand; sometimes it was veiled by long coarse grass. Huge skulls and whitening bones of buffalo were scattered everywhere. . . .'

Faced with the challenge of the Great Plains, the inventive American mind came up with solutions that were to win the vast area from the warrior Indians, the savage Apaches and Comanches, and from the Spaniards. To outdo the Mexican *vaquero* and mounted cavalry of the Apaches, the Americans developed the Colt six-shooter in the hands of the cowboy and the United States Cavalry. To cross the sea-like grasslands, the Pennsylvania covered wagon was developed into the prairie schooner, drawn by mules, horses, or oxen. Eventually, to contain the unrestricted roaming of herds across the prairies, barbed wire was to be introduced and, finally, irrigation and crops.

But the plains seemed at first no more than a barrier before the lush Pacific slopes, rather as Columbus had once seen the Americas as no more than an obstacle before China. Thus the hardiest of the pioneers leap-frogged the plains and clambered over the Rockies in the wake of Lewis and Clark; Oregon was settled before Montana, for Oregon provided the water and timber which the pioneer farmers had left behind and sought again. Clusters of American settlers began to till the soil of the Pacific coast in the Northwest and were on the spot to dispute the area with British and French-Canadian and even Russian fur-traders. Small groups of pioneers established themselves along the Oregon Trail, and squatters also reached northern California around Sutter's Fort and southern California along the Spanish trail through Santa Fe. Spanish government in New Mexico and California was venal and the American pioneers did not find it difficult to buy land and settle.

Westward expansion continued: some travelled in the comparative luxury of a horse-drawn wagon (*below right*); others walked (*below left*).

Yet for all this, much of the West was still uncharted. Grand Canyon (*above*) was virtually unknown till Joseph C. Ives's expedition of 1857–8.

James Monroe
by Gilbert Stuart.

While the first American pioneers were overcoming the droughts and blizzards of nature to reach the Pacific, the government in Washington was, as yet, unready to claim the continent as far as the Pacific. The Louisiana Purchase had not yet been settled. As always, American policy dragged behind the footsteps of the pioneers. With the collapse of the pro-British Federalists in face of the nationalism stirred up by the second war against England, Madison could pass on the White House to another Virginian, his Secretary of State, James Monroe. Monroe was a 'plain quiet man'; if his soul were turned inside out, Jefferson said, not a spot would be found on it. His retiring nature made him nearly invisible as a person, although he produced a doctrine in foreign policy that keeps his name evergreen. Domestically he did little, despite the fact that there was a large slump in 1819 due to the collapse of the war boom in New England and to over-speculation in western lands. Monroe had all the *laissez faire* attitudes of the Virginia dynasty, which thought that a man should be free to run his own plantation – if he had one. Yet Monroe did round off the southern flank of the United States by purchasing Florida from Spain, after Madison had encouraged settlers there to make government impossible for the Spaniards. A newspaper of the time showed American self-confidence by commenting that the Floridas 'naturally belong to us as the county of Cornwall does to England'. Monroe also warned the old régimes of Europe, which had crushed the

French Revolution and the constitutional government of Spain, to keep their hands off the Americas, even if the United States did not have the force to back up its warning.

The Monroe Doctrine of 1823 confirmed the policy that Jefferson had begun. The destiny of the United States lay in westward expansion and leadership in its own continent. If it left Europe alone, it might expect Europe to leave it alone. With British spindles becoming dependent on American cotton and British manufacturers needing the American market to absorb their goods, there was every reason to suppose that the British fleet would help to keep other European powers out of the Americas, where a rash of in-dependent republics had broken out with the collapse of the old empires of Spain and Portugal.

It was more profitable to trade with the Americas than to colonize them, because colonies cost money to rule and swallowed up a trading surplus. So Monroe's assertion, that the United States would not permit Europe to found new colonies in the Americas or interfere in the internal affairs of the

Loading a cotton steamer. From an engraving, c. 1860.

The fantastic rate of urban expansion in the nineteenth century is most dramatically illustrated by the growth of San Francisco. Hutton's drawing shows San Francisco in 1847.

American republics or transfer any European possessions in the New World to another power, suited the new commercial policy of England fairly well. In fact, agreement over the Canadian-American boundaries and the extinction of British hopes on the western plains allowed something of an 'era of good feelings' to begin between the two traditional enemies whose struggles had given each a respect for the quality of the other.

Yet the consequences of the Louisiana Purchase and the slump of 1819 now erupted to put an end to the complacent rule of the Virginia dynasty. There had been much Northern and Western discontent about the admission of Missouri as a slave state to the Union; it was balanced by the admission of Maine as a free state and by an agreement that no land in the Louisiana Purchase north of Missouri would allow slavery. Despite this warning of disaffection which Jefferson thought rang 'like a firebell in the night', Monroe managed to hand on the White House to a Northerner, his Secretary of State, John Quincy Adams. Adams succeeded only after a deadlock in the

San Francisco in 1852, after the Gold Rush. In five short years the town had expanded beyond recognition. Many of the clippers in the harbour were left to rot as their crews joined in the Rush.

Electoral College, which was ended by the House of Representatives pre-ferring him to the man who had won the most popular votes in the election of 1824, Andrew Jackson. The hero of New Orleans, called 'Old Hickory' because it was the toughest thing his troops knew, had won a large following, especially in the expanding West. Adams reached the White House as the people's second choice and the people were no longer content with aristo-cratic rule. Moreover, Adams came from the declining state of Massachusetts – upstart Ohio, the future mother of Presidents, already had a larger population of emigrants from New England and the South.

Adams in office was a mere caretaker for Andrew Jackson, as his father had been for Washington. His support eroded beneath him as the old colonial society that had survived the Revolution split and worked apart. He could well say of his four years' term, that it was 'a harassing, wearying, teasing condition of existence', nothing but 'perpetual motion and crazing cares', the weight of which 'grew heavier from day to day'.

The first cotton gin.

Chapter Three

THE COMING OF DEMOCRACY

The society under strain, which Adams failed to represent or lead, was *Expansion* undergoing the social revolution which the Constitution and the Virginia dynasty had postponed for forty years. The growth of factories in New England, of ports on the Atlantic, of cotton in the Southern economy, and of population in the West had disturbed the usual patterns of power. Large wage-earning groups of men and girls now filled the towns of New England near the source of water-power which drove the looms; employers' corporations began to develop the techniques of big business. Between the 1780s and the 1820s the states had grown from thirteen to twenty-four in number, population had increased three times and wealth four times. Seven cities now contained more than 50,000 people; another sixteen, including such cities in the new West as Cincinnati and its suburbs, held 25,000 or more. The cotton gin had made the cleaning and baling of cotton simple; the result was a boom in exports, plantations, and slaves. The hungry mouths of England's industrial workers demanded American grain. Western farmers had become geared to the markets of Eastern cities and of Europe; a slump in industry would bring a slump in farming. The old self-sufficiency of the farm was gone in the new sprawl of communications.

Canals and turnpikes, mainly financed by British capital, had begun to open up the West, with New York as the chief beneficiary. It sucked in goods along the new Erie Canal and offered frequent auctions and the regular sailings of Atlantic packets to keep goods moving through its warehouses. The ports to north and south of New York also prospered, but slowly, slowly. Only New Orleans boomed as much, with the Mississippi steamboats serving as the constant carriers of its wealth.

◀ A levee at New Orleans.

The expanding economy needed communications: turnpikes (*above*) and canals. The Erie Canal (*below*), which connects Lake Erie with the Hudson River, and thereby New York, was opened in 1825.

Robert Fulton's *Clermont*, launched in 1807, revolutionized shipping in America. Though by no means the first steamboat, it was the first to be a financial success.

The expanding West was the chief unsettler of old ways. In the North-west, there were still a few of the Mountain Men, who had blazed the trails to California in search of fur and who fed on raw buffalo innards; they were wilder than the Indians and ungovernable; 'they had little fear of God and none at all of the devil.' They had left something of their savage independence to the squatters who settled in their tracks, and these followers were many. Young men, and soon young women, deserted the Atlantic colonies; would-be planters pushed out with their slaves from their eroded lands in search of virgin soil – as Jefferson had said, the Americans found it cheaper to clear a new acre than to manure an old one. The Southern plantation system spread up to Missouri and across to Spanish Texas, while free farming moved west to Michigan and down to Kansas and Missouri to conflict with the slave-owners.

'A mighty spreading and shifting' took place in the West. In this ferment old ideas and restraints dissolved and new ones were spawned. Equality of opportunity seemed real when there was so little cash available and so much land. 'Good land, dog-cheap everywhere, or for nothing, if you will go for it,' one observer wrote, 'gives as much elbow-room to every man as he chooses

'The Follies of the Age, Vive le Humbug'. A lithograph, c. 1850.

Zank you Mérican peoples—I gif you fifty dollar for Lunatic Asylum and I expect you gif me back fifty tousand dollar.

MAIL STEAMERS FOR LIVERPOOL

While I engage your Master in conversation you will have a fine chance to escape

to take.' Even if the liberty of men to own land meant the slavery of their wives to sod huts and the loss of all civilization, yet in the small towns behind the frontier, the first leisure given to women by the new riches of their husbands meant a brouhaha of ideas. Speculation in land was matched by speculation in theories; the fads of the distant cities became the meat of those bored by small-town life or discouraged by drudgery to the soil. Revivalism swept over Upper New York State and Ohio; primitive Christianity gave the South the religious shakes. Temperance, spiritualism, magnetism, gymnastics, cold-water cures, physiology, and even anti-slavery and women's rights found their supporters in the innovating back country. The Westerners, by good demands and bad, were making the government hear them. 'No sooner do you set foot upon American ground,' de Tocqueville declared in 1831, 'than you are stunned by a kind of tumult; a confused clamour is heard on every side, and a thousand simultaneous voices demand the satisfaction of their social wants.'

Outside New England there was a feeling of frustration. The Supreme Court, headed by John Marshall, had asserted itself against federal and state governments, declaring tax laws against the individual or the corporation unconstitutional. Yet the Westerners wanted the old states to pay more taxes to finance better canals and roads to the new states. The textile factories of New England demanded high tariffs to protect the home market against cheap English goods; such a policy drove up the price of clothing for the Western farmer, whose crop prices were not protected. The planters of Virginia and the brahmins of Massachusetts had held a monopoly on the White House; it was time for a change. The expectation of a millennium in the New World was everywhere in the air, even in the back country of the

79

old Atlantic states. 'Poor mother earth was never so beat and exercised as now,' a self-made reformer from New York wrote in 1825, 'and she must think a new race dwells on her surface.'

That new race put Andrew Jackson in the White House in 1828 by a popular vote. He won a majority in all the states of the West and the South and split the Middle Atlantic states with John Quincy Adams, who carried only New England. Jackson succeeded in capturing the working-men's vote in New York City and Philadelphia by seeming to be the candidate of the poor against the privileged. Thus the founder of the Democratic Party set the pattern for its later victories – a stitching together of the vote of the discontented agrarians in the South and the West with the labour vote in the Northern cities. Jackson's campaign typed the new Democratic Party as the party of the underdog and the debtor, however reactionary some of its policies might be because of the influence of its Southern wing.

Jackson won the election because he put into flesh the hope of the majority. He incarnated the man of iron, self-made and obstinate and daring, the model of the businessman and frontiersman. 'Of all the men I have known,' a friend said, 'Andrew Jackson was the one most entirely sufficient for himself', and for the many who would have liked to have been him. In a time of expectant capitalism, when a fortune seemed within the grasp of any resolute man, Jackson was the brawling yet compelling President, 'one of nature's noblemen', who had forced himself upwards from modest beginnings. 'This is a country of self-made men', a contemporary wrote, 'than which nothing better could be said of any state of society.'

Jackson's successes and mistakes in office were part and parcel of his belief, not in the common man, but in the uncommon man who could make himself rich through hard work. Jackson entrenched the spoils system in American politics to reform the abuse of power; he believed that any man of good will could do any bureaucratic job, that long tenure corrupted, and that quick change in office was a form of healthy competition. He attacked and finally destroyed the Second Bank of the United States not only because Western farmers made it into the scapegoat of foreclosed mortgages, but also because small businessmen wanted easy money for mushroom growth. When a Jacksonian Senator denounced the Bank, it was because it mortgaged 'all the flourishing *cities* of the West'.

The head of the Bank, Nicholas Biddle, was a man whose arrogance

Nicholas Biddle. matched Jackson's own, and Jackson brooked no rival. He destroyed

Biddle's power over the economy and Congress just as he had destroyed the British at New Orleans. 'The Bank', he declared to his Vice-President and successor, Van Buren, 'is trying to kill me, *but I will kill it*.' The consequence of destroying the Bank and of depositing surplus federal revenue in favoured state banks was to whip the spiral of speculation into a tornado of greed, which devastated the landscape and America's credit when Van Buren inherited Jackson's place.

Other measures by Jackson played into the hands of the speculators, however much he hated them as a breed. His policy of exterminating the Indians ruthlessly opened up more lands to exploitation. His veto of federal aid to build a turnpike across Kentucky killed off Western hopes of cheap 'internal improvements' and left the development of transport in the hands of Eastern financiers who would later provoke rural revolts against their power. Jackson's acceptance of high tariffs further helped the industrialists and forced up prices for the Westerners; he also kept the prices of public lands high to the disappointment of his supporters. He wanted a large federal surplus to pay off the national debt, which he succeeded in doing; but his action only put more money in the hands of the few who had chosen to speculate in government bonds.

If many of Jackson's deeds helped his enemies and provoked his friends, yet he showed himself strong in what he called his 'situation of dignified slavery'. When the Supreme Court made a decision in favour of the Cherokee Indians, whom Jackson hated, he refused to carry it out, saying: 'John Marshall has made his decision; now let him enforce it.' When Calhoun took South Carolina to the point of secession over the high tariff policy, Jackson deterred the revolt by the threat of force and the toast: 'Our Federal Union, it must be preserved.' He used the veto power of the Presidency more often than all the previous Presidents put together, once declaring that he 'would receive no message from the damned scoundrels' in the Senate. His contempt for Congress and authoritarian use of the presidential power offended the rich, who had local power, and the Senate. These looked for a figurehead to replace this popular general who acted as President to the full.

De Tocqueville noticed that there were no Parties during Jackson's first term in the White House, because the Federalists were ruined and Jackson first called his Party the Democratic Republicans, thus engulfing all opposition outside a few factions. The Jacksonians were not to be called simply Democrats until Jackson himself stepped down. In fact, de Tocqueville found such dominance by the people that even the ex-Federalists and the rich submitted to democracy as an irremediable evil. 'But beneath this artificial enthusiasm and these obsequious attentions to the preponderating power', de Tocqueville warned, 'it is easy to perceive that the rich have a hearty dislike of the democratic institutions of their country. The people form a power which they at once fear and despise.' The privileged had to found a Party of their own to fight the Democratic Party within the popular system; the Federalists had foundered in treason and secession. Thus the Whig Party was born, and soon adopted the system of nominating a presidential candidate at a national convention, where states were represented by delegates.

Henry Clay tried to run against Jackson in 1832 for a group called the National Republicans and was heavily defeated. While Jackson made an emotional appeal to the poor against the Bank, Clay tried to present his 'American System' rationally. 'We must keep the two interests of domestic manufactures and internal improvements allied', he declared, suggesting a future winning combination of Northern and Western interests. Yet he also stood for a strong Congress and a weak President. 'We are in the midst of a revolution, hitherto bloodless, but rapidly tending towards a total change of the pure republican character of the government, and to the concentration of all power in the hands of one man.' The powers of Congress were being paralysed under this 'elective monarchy – the worst of all forms of government'.

So Henry Clay warned that Jackson was doing what Washington had refused to do; but Jackson stepped down and handed over to Van Buren, an efficient machine politician from New York with none of the powers of command of 'Old Hickory'. Van Buren won the election of 1836 against a divided opposition, for the new Whig Party could not yet unite the National Republicans and Anti-Masons and other enemies of the Democrats; but the Whig candidate, General William Henry Harrison, Virginia born and resident in Ohio, showed how another Party could steal Jackson's thunder. Harrison was an undistinguished man, far inferior to such Senators as Clay; but he was an Indian-slaying general. Doubters might ask: 'If New Orleans in all its fame of truth, should furnish no civic wreath to the victor, can Tippecanoe supply it?' But emotional appeals proved winning ones in the new democracy of American politics and Harrison crushed Van Buren in 1840 by preaching the virtues of log-cabins and hard cider – buildings he seldom set foot in, and a drink that he rarely touched. Van Buren suffered for the consequences of the depression caused by Jackson's economic policies and was laughed out of office to the campaign jingle of:

Little Van, Van, Van, Van
Oh! He's a used-up man!

Harrison's only act as President before he quickly expired was to pen the doctrine of the weak Executive which the Whig Senators wanted. 'It is preposterous to suppose that a thought could for a moment have been entertained that the President, placed at the capital, in the centre of the country, could better understand the wants and wishes of the people than their own immediate representatives, who spend a part of every year among them, living with them, often labouring with them, and bound to them by the triple tie of interest, duty and affection.' So much for the Jacksonian idea of the President as the direct voice of the people. Harrison was the first of a long line of Presidents from Ohio, whose weakness in the White House was exceeded only by their ambition to get there.

Henry Clay.

Martin van Buren.

The new President, John Tyler from Virginia, was the first Vice-President to step into a dead man's shoes. He was a conservative and he would have liked to be a strong President; but he was blocked by Congress. Once the Senate had found it could have a weak President, it would knuckle under only to the strongest of Chief Executives. Moreover, the divisions of the continent had made for rising tempers in Congress; the 'peculiar institution' of slavery had begun to rend the normal institutions of the United States.

Slavery   Slavery was becoming outdated. The British had abolished the slave trade in 1807, preferring morality to profits; gradually the old régimes of Europe were doing away with the last vestiges of serfdom. Yet the southern states held their black people in bondage. Once the Virginia legislature had decided to keep slavery after the bloody revolt of some Negroes under Nat Turner in 1831, all opposition to slavery became stilled in the South. Those sickened by the system left for free land in the West; but King Cotton and its profits provided a reason to let slaves be and breed. The production of cotton increased seventeenfold between 1820 and 1860, making the South largely dependent on one crop; the slave population also increased two and a half times to some 3,500,000 in these decades, despite the fact that one Negro baby in two died.

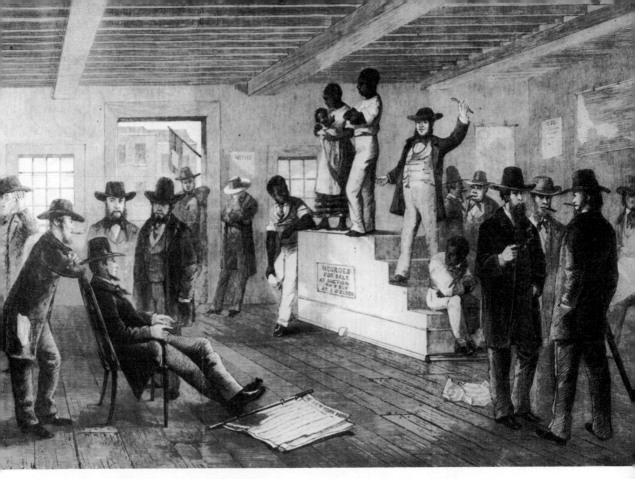

The sad reality of the slave auction (*above*) contrasts with the idealized view of the Negro's lot (*opposite*). The invention of the cotton gin sent soaring the prices paid for slaves.

Curiously enough, only a minority of Southern white farmers actually had slaves, and the competition of slave labour made poor white farmers even poorer; yet opposition to 'the great central nerve of slavery' came to seem treason to the South, a criticism 'so dangerous that none but a madman would risk it'. A visiting Northerner explained the poor whites' point of view by writing that 'the one thing in their condition which has made life valuable to the mass of whites has been that the niggers are yet their inferiors. . . . That is deemed to be the chief blessing of slavery.' Moreover, Southerners could accuse Northern industrialists such as the 'Boston Associates' of turning the millions of immigrant Irish and Germans into wage-slaves for their machines, and permitting an even more bestial life in urban slums than in plantation shacks.

Countless thousands emigrated from Europe in general, and Ireland (*below left*) in particular. But the nearest many of them came to a promised land of opportunity was semi-slavery in a Northern factory.

The West, as usual, provoked the quarrel between North and South. The passionate few evangelists, who denounced slavery as a denial of the American promise of liberty and equality for all, suddenly found that their converts in the Midwest had gone to war. In a long series of skirmishes, the Free Soilers raided and were raided by slave-owners across the Midwest. Revivalism stirred the righteousness of those struggling for control of the governments of the new western territories and states. Both supporters and opponents of slavery used the Bible to justify their position. And the states of the old South, falling more and more in debt to New York and London financiers, pinned their last hopes of influence in the national councils on the trinity of cotton and slaves and aristocratic talents of command.

As the western frontier became tamed, Southern Senators watched jealously the number of free states admitted to the Union, in order to match each anti-slavery state with a slave one. Thus when the Democrat James Polk of Tennessee became President in 1845 – a man so self-willed that he earned the name of 'Young Hickory' – they backed his policy of expansion in the Southwest, chiefly populated by Americans from the old South. Polk was to complete what Jefferson had begun and Jackson now euphemistically

Manifest
Destiny

Living conditions for workers were often extremely primitive.

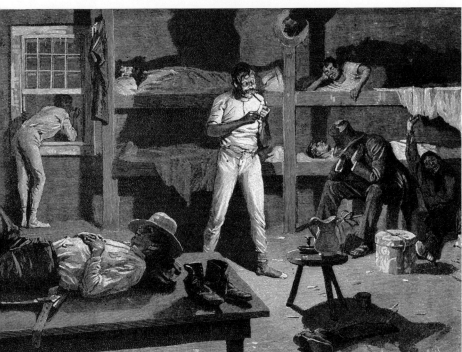

87

called 'extending the area of freedom'; he took the expansion of the United States to the Pacific by annexing the Southwest and dividing the Northwest with Britain. In fact, the grabbing of the Southwest was what Harriet Martineau called it, 'the most high-handed theft of modern times'. It is strange that expansion over a continent can be excused as 'Manifest Destiny' or the extension of freedom, while expansion across an ocean becomes tyranny or imperialism.

Polk went to war to annex the West. Tyler's last act in office had been to annex Texas, which had already declared itself an independent republic after the famous victory of Sam Houston and the American immigrants over the Mexican army of Santa Anna at San Jacinto. He feared that the English might blandish the independent Texans into an alliance to keep the Westerners off the Pacific coast. There had been many recent skirmishes between the Americans and the Canadians along the border and in the Northwest; Polk had won much Western support by promising to annex the whole of the Northwest, even if it meant fighting Britain. Once in office, however, he settled for a division of the Northwest along the line of the forty-ninth parallel, leaving British Columbia in the hands of the Canadians. While Mexico was weak, Britain was strong, and Polk could not afford a two-front war. Moreover, both Westerners and Southerners would support a war for the Southwest, while the Northerners might threaten secession again if another war with England ruined their trade.

Despite the reluctance of the North, Polk found enough support to fight Mexico. He ran the war personally from the White House, using the President's powers as commander-in-chief to raise money from Congress and direct operations. He sent an army under General Zachary Taylor to occupy the Southwest, while General Winfield Scott was ordered to invade the interior of Mexico and occupy its capital. A humiliating peace was imposed on the Mexican government; the Southwest was bought at the point of a bayonet for a mere $18,250,000. By the Oregon Treaty and the Mexican War Polk had added another third to the land area of the United States and had made his country straddle its continent. Even if the Americans had not expanded over the whole northern hemisphere of the Americas, they fronted two oceans. The internal problem of slavery now turned many of the aggressive instincts of the United States inwards; the symptoms of Civil War and convalescence from the disease would prevent further attacks on outside enemies for half a century.

General Winfield Scott marching into Mexico City in 1848. Thirteen years later, though a Virginian, General Scott commanded the Union armies for the first few months of the Civil War.

The abolition of slavery could not pass the Senate, as long as one-third of the Senators came from slave-holding states and could block a constitutional amendment. Thus the moderates of North and South sought for accommodation in the West. By the Compromise of 1850 California was admitted as a free state, while the rest of the Mexican cession was opened up to slavery, if the settlers decided to have slaves. The matter was to be decided by the race to the West of migrants from North and South. A Fugitive Slave Law was also passed to satisfy the Southerners that runaways would always be returned; but, in fact, the law was nullified in the Northeast, where fervent abolitionists openly helped Negroes to escape along the 'underground rail-road' to Canada. Another compromise, the Kansas-Nebraska Act, set aside the Missouri Compromise that had banned slavery north of the border of that state. It turned over the question of slavery to local squatters; but thousands of slave-owners crossed into Kansas to vote in a pro-slavery government, only to be attacked by bands of Northern abolitionists such as the fanatic John Brown. Open warfare broke out in 'Bleeding Kansas'; terror was used by slave-owner and abolitionist alike.

The Kansas-Nebraska Act

89

An early railroad station. Note the Indians waiting for a train.

The South had become desperate to create new slave states to counter/balance the free territories of the Northwest that would soon ask to become states. Thus it pushed the government to found new slave states in Cuba and Central America, in tropical climates suitable for growing cotton by the plantation system. Manifest Destiny threatened to overspill the natural boundaries of the United States, all because of the internal tensions bred by slavery. In fact, further extension of Jackson's 'area of freedom' meant an extension of the area of bondage.

The South had reason to fear, for the North and West had fallen into an economic alliance. Despite the Gadsden Purchase of another slice of the Southwest to make an intercontinental railroad possible along a Southern route, Northern rail interests were far advanced in binding the West to New England by iron ties. Twenty/one thousand miles of track were laid in the 1850s, making Chicago the funnel through which Western goods had to pour to the Northeast. This huge development was made possible by the corruption of politicians, who granted 25,000,000 acres of free land to the railroads to finance their operations. Until the slump of 1857, the booming states of the West consumed the goods of New England and paid with their food crops. In the twenty years before 1860, Ohio, Michigan, Illinois,

Indiana, and Wisconsin trebled their production of food and doubled their population. The area and power of the free farming system grew faster than that of the plantation system; individual hope and greed developed the land far more efficiently than forced labour. Money was nearly all, and, despite the fortunes made by the few from King Cotton, most of the money was made by businessmen and farmers in the North and the West. 'In America,' Emerson noted, 'out of doors, all seems a market, indoors, an air-tight stove of conventionalism.'

What was conventional in the North and West, however, was the system of free enterprise, and the convention was in direct conflict with the traditional slavery of the South. Although many Southerners emigrated west, they failed to match the emigration of the Yankees and the German and Scandinavian farmers who came through Northern ports and picked up Yankee ideas. The abolitionist followed the Methodist and Baptist preacher out to the Midwest above Missouri and found consciences to stir. Many Yankees considered that their own rights of free speech and assembly and protest were threatened if the South tried to muzzle all attacks on slavery. As a female abolitionist wrote of the slave: 'In striving to strike his irons off, we found most surely, that *we* were manacled *ourselves*.'

A special train taking American and European dignitaries (much of the capital was raised in Europe) to celebrate the completion of the North Pacific Railroad on 8 September 1883.

Harriet Beecher Stowe, author of *Uncle Tom's Cabin*, and Chief Justice Roger B. Taney, who, though he had manumitted his own slaves, destroyed the Missouri Compromise by his judgment in the Dred Scott case of 1857.

The Dred Scott Case   The publication of *Uncle Tom's Cabin* in 1852 made the sufferings of the slave known in every household in the land. When the five Southern Justices in the Supreme Court declared in the Dred Scott case that a slave remained a slave even in a free state, anger against the South boiled over. John Brown attacked the federal arsenal at Harpers Ferry to seize weapons and arm a slave revolt; he was captured by troops led by the Virginia Colonel Robert E. Lee and hanged. Fury had spilled over into guerilla war. Only the firmest of Presidents and Parties could cope with such a crisis of economics and incidents.

Polk left the Democrats divided; the Party creed had come out openly for slavery by dropping the slave-owning Jefferson's Declaration of Independence. As Abraham Lincoln from Illinois commented later, the Democrats had taken the position that one man's liberty was absolutely nothing when it conflicted with another man's property. Van Buren, still anxious to return to the White House, ran in 1848 and won enough anti-slavery Democratic votes from the official Party candidate to let in the Whig nominee, General Zachary Taylor of Louisiana, who imitated General Harrison so faithfully as military hero and political putty that he also died in office. The Vice-

This photograph of John Brown, taken around 1856, betrays his 'touch of insanity'. He was executed in 1859, after his attack on Harpers Ferry.

President, Millard Fillmore from New York, was as insignificant as his predecessor. The next two Presidents improved on Fillmore only up to the level of the mediocre; these were Franklin Pierce from New Hampshire and James Buchanan from Pennsylvania. Both were Democrats and both were 'dough-faces', pro-slavery Northerners who tried to save Party and Union by a policy of drift towards the cataract.

The inadequacy of the leaders of the Whigs and the Democrats led to the splintering of the old Parties. The massive immigration of the Roman Catholic Irish, fleeing from famine and British rule, led to the toadstool growth of the nativist Know-Nothing Party, dedicated to nationalism and anti-Catholicism. Fillmore agreed to head its presidential ticket in 1856 and won more than one vote in five; but, despite local successes, its poisonous growth quickly rotted away. Virulent nativism erupts and diminishes in regular cycles in American life; the excesses of primitive nationalism are soon succeeded by shame at those excesses. Europe and its immigrants and influences are often the whipping-boy for America's ills; yet the backs and brains of aliens from across the Atlantic have helped to build America. In the two decades before 1860, the 17,000,000 Americans swelled to

31,500,000; New York City alone held more than a million people. This new population toiled for the industrial and agricultural expansion of the continent; but the fact that much of it arrived by steerage put still further strains on the strained pattern of the old.

The Republican Party

The fragmentation of political life called up a new Party with an old name, the Republicans. They were originally a 'party of moral ideas', which explains why they never lost all the reformers within their ranks even when big business later dominated the Party. Above all, they had one moral idea about the Union, summed up by Lincoln: 'It will become all one thing, or all the other. Either the opponents of slavery will arrest the further spread of it . . . or its advocates will push it forward till it should become alike lawful in all the States, old as well as new, North as well as South.' Slavery was an aggressive institution, faced by the aggressive capitalism of the North. While the North imported the cheap labour of immigrants, the South bred the cheap labour of slaves. The one stood against the other. 'If free Negroes should be made *things*,' Lincoln asked, 'how long, think you, before they will begin to make *things* out of poor white men?' The virgin lands of the West should be 'an outlet for free white people everywhere, the world over'; and this could not be, 'to any considerable extent, if slavery shall be planted within them'.

Slaves working in a cottonfield.

The works of the Paterson Iron Company. In a drawn-out struggle, the industrial North was almost bound to defeat the predominantly agricultural South.

John Frémont.

Thus the Republicans turned the morality of the abolitionists into the practical problem of keeping the flow of free whites into the Western lands and Northern factories. Negro slaves, after all, were not in a position to consume many manufactured goods; the single crop of the cotton economy left much land to waste; the Southern individualist character opposed co-operative efforts for internal improvements. The Republicans significantly chose as their first presidential candidate in 1856 the Far Western explorer, soldier, and Governor of California Territory, John C. Frémont. He beat the Whigs into third place, carrying the anti-slavery areas. To have a chance of winning next time, the Republicans only had to nominate someone with both a wider and a more cautious programme, 'a Tariff, River-and-Harbour, Pacific Railroad, Free-Homestead man'. This was Abraham Lincoln.

95

Chapter Four

CIVIL WAR, RECONSTRUCTION AND REUNION

The break-down of the old Parties led directly to the Civil War, because the traditional politicians were not prepared to accept government at the hands of a raw Party from nowhere and a gangling politician from Illinois, who had not even the saving grace of being a victorious general. Lincoln had really risen from log-cabin and working origins to capture the Republican nomination in 1860; he was a humble man of the people, even if he had breathed and eaten politics all his life. But his ambition was 'a little engine that knew no rest'.

The slavery question split the Democrats, so that the Southern Democrats nominated a pro-slavery candidate and the Northern Democrats chose the sponsor of the Kansas-Nebraska Act, Stephen Douglas, who had beaten Lincoln in a senatorial race in 1858. Lincoln gathered the support of the decayed Know-Nothings and of moderates in the North. He carefully made no statements demanding the emancipation of the slaves; on the other hand, he declared that slavery was a wrong – something that neither Democratic candidate would do. Although Lincoln won only two votes in five, he carried all the populous Northern states and part of the West, winning a clear majority in the Electoral College. Except for Virginia and Missouri, the South stayed behind the Southern Democratic candidate and refused to accept this sectional verdict against its peculiar institution.

The leader in the Southern movement for secession was, naturally, South Carolina. It had been humbled by the Force Act once passed against it by the Western people's candidate, Jackson; although later he had begun to

Abraham Lincoln.

lower the tariff to appease the nullifying state, yet he had left rebellious memories. Precedents for secession were many. Some of the New England states had followed the original example of Virginia and Kentucky in their Resolutions to the very brink of secession; if they had stepped back, it was because their fears had been allayed by a change in government policy or electoral fortune. But nothing could remove the Southern fear of Lincoln and the 'Black Republican Party', that these men had been elected to undo slavery – which they had. 'The ruin of the South, by the emancipation of her slaves,' a Charleston newspaper wrote with a fine gloss upon the meaning of freedom, 'is the loss of liberty, property, home, country – everything that makes life worth having.'

So Lincoln's victory began the serious movement of secession in the South. Just before his assassination, Lincoln himself best summed up the chain of events leading up to the Civil War: 'Both parties deprecated war, but one of them would *make* war rather than let the nation survive, and the other would *accept* war rather than let it perish, and the war came.' The

Jefferson Davis.

coming was slow, as the South heaped provocation after provocation upon Lincoln.

The Southerners could not trust Lincoln to let slavery be – how could he, as a Republican? Before his inauguration, South Carolina had been followed by Georgia and the five states on the Gulf of Mexico into a declaration of secession. A Government of the Confederate States of America was set up with Jefferson Davis of Misssssippi as its provisional President. Yet Virginia and other southern states away from the Gulf hesitated; without their support secession would be futile, even if Southern fire-eaters dreamt that King Cotton must win. Did not the looms of Britain depend on cotton? Did not cotton make up two-thirds by value of all American exports, to the tune of $1,768,000,000 in 1860? To Southern extremists, victory over the North was sure, with the British bound to intervene on their side; this would be the prelude to expansion all over the Americas. Such wishful thinking merely fed Northern fears of a Southern conspiracy to found a 'slave empire' throughout the New World.

While the South armed, Lincoln decided that he would make a symbolic show of federal authority. The government held two forts in the South, one of which was Fort Sumter dominating Charleston harbour. Despite demands from South Carolina, the federal commander in Sumter decided to hold out until Lincoln sent in provisions to him, although not arms.

After a thirty-four-hour bombardment, Major Robert Anderson surrendered Fort Sumter to General Beauregard. Surprisingly enough no one was killed in the fighting!

General Beauregard, who commanded the local troops, decided to attack and capture Sumter, treating Lincoln's provisioning of the fort as a definite military threat. Lincoln's action was hardly provocative if weighed against Southern attacks on his authority as President; yet his decision not to surrender all federal authority in the South led to the assault on Sumter, for the South Carolinians could hardly allow a federal fort to bottle up their best harbour.

Fort Sumter

The result of the firing on Sumter was to unite the hesitant North behind Lincoln and the Union in a 'patriotic storm'. One Northerner wrote, 'We drifted. Now the rudder is felt.' Even Douglas supported Lincoln and urged the Northern Democrats to enlist against the South, which had declared 'a war of aggression' against the 'Government established by our fathers'. There was no complex choice to be made; there were '*only patriots – or traitors*'. Similar simplifications led to Virginia, North Carolina, Tennessee, and Arkansas throwing in their lot with the slave states.

After capturing Vicksburg in 1863, Grant (*above*) drove Lee towards Richmond. At Petersburg Lee made a last desperate stand, but the Union forces (*left*) broke through on 2 April 1865.

Civil War

Goliath was on the side of the Union; 22,500,000 people and most of the means of war production stood behind Lincoln. The Confederacy had only 5,500,000 whites and 3,500,000 slaves whom it could not arm; it was pitiably short of industry and strategic materials. One American in fifty was to die in the four bloody years to follow. The Union was able to raise twice the number of men and twice the amount of real money available to the South; it also had the shipyards to equip squadrons to blockade the South, dependent on imports for many war necessities. The best hope of the South was a quick victory; its long resistance was a tribute to its stubborn beliefs and its soldiers' courage.

The Confederates had the best general in the war, Robert E. Lee (*above*), but his soldiers (*left*), though brave and enduring, were always short of equipment and supplies.

The South had an immediate advantage over the North because its planters were a born officer class and its poor whites were used to hunting with rifles and living on inferior rations. Robert E. Lee was the best general on either side, although his failure to take Washington, despite a series of victories or drawn battles with a succession of stubborn Union generals, gradually wore away the South's inferior forces in a war of attrition to defend Lee's home state. The battles of Bull Run, Antietam, Fredericksburg, Chancellorsville, Gettysburg were useless massacres in or near that Virginia which had once given its leading citizens to be strong Presidents of a strong Union.

By the time Lee surrendered (*right*), the combined death-roll had reached the appalling figure of 650,000 (compared with 400,000 American dead in the Second World War) in a population of only 30,000,000. Union casualties (*centre*) were fifty per cent higher than those of the Confederates (*top*).

SURRENDER OF GEN. LEE!

"The Year of Jubilee has come! Let all the People Rejoice!"

200 GUNS WILL BE FIRED

On the Campus Martius,

AT 3 O'CLOCK TO-DAY, APRIL 10,

To Celebrate the Victories of our Armies.

Every Man, Woman and Child is hereby ordered to be on hand prepared to Sing and Rejoice. The crowd are expected to join in singing Patriotic Songs.

ALL PLACES OF BUSINESS MUST BE CLOSED AT 2 O'CLOCK.

Hurrah for Grant and his noble Army.

By Order of the People.

Lee's army laying down its arms, April 1865.

Meanwhile, the Union was winning the war in the West and on the Mississippi. Admiral Farragut did what the British had failed to do; he captured New Orleans in 1862. General Ulysses S. Grant cleared the Mississippi River next year after his brilliant capture of Vicksburg. When he was transferred to oppose Lee in the East, he used his superior forces to batter Lee backwards towards Richmond, the Confederate capital, while General Sherman cut the South in two by harrying his way through to Georgia. In April 1865, the surrounded Lee was forced to surrender the last of the Confederate forces at Appomattox Court House.

General Sherman.

ASSASSINATIO
OF
PRESIDENT
L'INCOLN

ATTEMPTED MURDER O
MR. SEWARD..

(REUTER'S TELEGRAMS.)
NEW YORK, APRIL 15 (10 A.M.)
At 1.30 this morning Mr. Stanton reported
follows :—
"This evening, at 9.30, President Lincol
while sitting in a private box at Ford's thea
with Mrs. Lincoln, Mrs. Harris, and Maj
Rathburn, was shot by an assassin, w
suddenly entered the box, and approach
behind the President. The assassin the
leaped upon the stage, brandishing a lar
knife and escaped in the rear of the theatr
A pistol ball entered the back of the Presiden
head, penetrating nearly through. The wour
is mortal.
"The President has been insensible ever sin
the infliction of the wound, and is now dying.

John Wilkes Booth's callous act did immeasurable harm to the South, for it gave Northern radicals a moral sanction for their policy of vengeance and repression.

Lincoln's conduct of the war did not equal his posthumous reputation. His policy was to preserve the Union, not to free the slave; in fact, early in the war he would have accepted the Confederacy back into the Union with slavery intact. For more than a year Lincoln resisted abolitionist demands to declare all slaves free, for he feared that the wavering border states of Maryland, Kentucky, Missouri, and Delaware might join the Confederacy if their slaves were emancipated. Freeing the slave was less a moral decision than a military one of trying to foment a Negro rebellion behind the Southern lines. There was also a political reason behind emancipation: if the unreformed South were allowed back into Congress, the situation would return to the hopeless deadlock of the 1850s.

At last, Lincoln signed an Emancipation Proclamation, fearful that, if the constitutional issue of the war were not made into a moral one, the English government might intervene on the side of the aristocratic Confederacy and ignore the antislavery sentiment of British working people. In fact, the Proclamation only freed the slaves in Confederate territory; slaves behind the Union lines remained in bondage. Lincoln's Proclamation had all the righteousness of a man who starts a fire to purify another's backyard.

A funeral service was held at the White House on 19 April, and Lincoln's body lay in state in the Capitol for two days.

Not until he won a second term in office by a comfortable majority over the Democrats led by his dismissed army chief, General McClellan, did Lincoln back the Thirteenth Amendment to the Constitution, which allowed 'neither slavery nor involuntary servitude' in the United States.

Lincoln was always more moderate than the bulk of his own Party, which became dominated by increasingly radical and speculative elements. He wanted 'to bind up the nation's wounds'; thus he chose as his running mate a Democrat, Andrew Johnson, from the officially Confederate state of Tennessee. The assassin's bullet which killed Lincoln just after the end of the Civil War may have made him, as the editor Horace Greeley wrote, 'the victim of a conspiracy of partisans of the Rebellion'; but it also made the defeated South the victim of a conspiracy of partisans of the radicals. The Republicans in Congress could now 'reconstruct' the South, unchecked by the martyred President; his corpse would be brandished to deny the moderation which his flesh and blood had practised. When the good a leader does is interred with his bones, the evil his Party does lives after him. It took the South one hundred years to forgive what the Republicans did in the name of Lincoln.

Mr Golightly on his way to California in 1849. In addition to that in California, there were gold rushes at Pike's Peak (1858–9), in South Dakota (1874–6) and the Klondike (1897).

Reconstruction

The United States certainly needed full-scale reconstruction after the Civil War. Huge new tariffs had encouraged the rapid growth of Northern industries and had helped to pay for the war; but inflation had halved the value of the dollar, while profiteering had created millionaires without spreading wealth. These millionaires rapidly corrupted the Republicans into the Party of big business and high tariffs, but the poor had to pay more for imported goods and monopolies. The Homestead Act of 1862 may have given 160 acres of free western land to anyone who would till it for five years, but it also encouraged speculators to take over government lands by using 'dummy settlers' to get title to a homestead after only six months of occupation at the low fixed price of $1.25 an acre. Another 70,000,000 acres went for nothing to three large railroads during the war, and much of the best land was reserved for education and the state and federal governments.

In fact, Lincoln and Congress seemed to encourage the Eastern business-man more than the Western small farmer. This was proved when the Republicans passed National Banking Acts to remove financial power from the states to Washington; centralized banking was now put together again after Jackson's assaults. A national currency and a large federal debt secured by California gold strengthened the Union's credit, while the South was reduced to beggary by Sherman's devastation and the loss of a billion dollars' worth or more of capital in the war.

The radical Republicans reconstructed little during Reconstruction. They left the West at the mercy of Eastern financiers whom they failed to curb. They inflicted an odious and corrupt government on the defeated South and reduced it to America's chief area of poverty for generations. When Andrew Johnson tried to assert his authority and treat the defeated Confederacy with some moderation, the Republicans, under Thaddeus Stevens, brought articles of impeachment against him, and failed to rid themselves of him by only one vote in the House of Representatives. It was true that the Confederate states took advantage of Johnson's early leniency to put their old leaders back in power and enact Black Codes, which sought to reduce the Southern Negro to a state akin to slavery once again; but the Black Codes hardly merited the brutal counter-attack of the radical Republicans.

Four important inventions of the first half of the nineteenth century: the steam printing press, the telegraph, the locomotive and the steamboat.

In fact, Congress used Reconstruction to try and dominate the Executive and the Supreme Court – a dream of introducing the British parliamentary system to the United States that has always tempted the American legislature. Johnson stupidly tried to fight the large radical Republican majority in Congress rather than compromise with it; he vetoed Bills for the continuance of the Republican pork barrel and political machine in the South, the Freedmen's Bureau, and for Civil Rights. Congress riposted by imposing military rule on the southern states without appeal to the Supreme Court, by ramming through the Fourteenth Amendment to ensure that no state should 'abridge the privileges or immunities of citizens of the United States' without losing some of its representation in Congress, and by initiating the Fifteenth Amendment to give all male American citizens the vote without 'account of race, colour, or previous condition of servitude'. (Half of the American adult population and half of the matriarchal slave society, those human beings who happened to be women, were ignored and told that they were hardly citizens.)

The election of General Grant from Ohio to the White House in 1868 confirmed the Republican solution to the peace. The Republicans put in the Union commander-in-chief by waving the bloody shirt. Soon the southern states came under the rule of freed Negroes who were often illiterate, of carpetbaggers from the North with an eye for ideals and loot, and of renegade white Southerners called 'scalawags'. Although the Reconstruction governments in the South did institute public education and railroad construction, heavy taxation ruined the plantation economy and brought in the sapping system of share-cropping and tenant-farming, by which a farmer never earned enough cash to run away from his slavery to the crops on his land. Bondage to an inescapable debt can nearly approach plantation slavery.

In fact, stubborn white resistance in the South and the use of terror against the Negroes by such organizations as the Ku Klux Klan broke the Republicans' will to impose Negro suffrage and one-party rule on society below the Potomac. Gradually, conservative and racist Democrats regained control of the governments of the southern states until, by 1877, a compromise was reached. Federal troops were withdrawn and white supremacy was recognized in the solid Democratic South, which in turn co-operated with the Eastern barons of big business, who controlled the Republican Party, rather than with the agrarian West.

Ku Klux Klan

◀ The inauguration of Ulysses S. Grant, 1869.

After the Civil War,
the Ku Klux Klan
began its
reign of terror.

Corruption and   The Republicans now refused to help the freed Negroes and to enforce
Compromise   suffrage for all under the threat of the Fourteenth Amendment; in return the
Southern Senators did not oppose the high tariffs demanded by the Republican
financiers. If the East would keep the federal government from allowing
Negroes to vote in the South, the South would keep the federal government
from regulating monopolies in the East. The bloody war was succeeded by a
cynical accommodation of interests, which gave to Northern millionaires
and Southern racists the wrong dearest to their hearts. This alliance between
conservative Republicans and conservative Southern Democrats was to
put a block in the Senate on almost every progressive President, until the
Texan Lyndon Johnson sat in the White House. Meanwhile, deserted by
their old political allies, the Negroes gradually sank back into an unofficial
serfdom to the eroding soil and into segregation from white society, both in
the Jim Crow South and in the black ghettoes of the Northern cities.

The corruption at Washington under Grant piled boodle on graft on
swag. Grant himself was an honest, dull man, who could lead soldiers by
the force of his will in war and who was led by the penchant of financiers for
profits in peace. 'The House of Representatives', an ex-Congressman wrote
at this time, 'was like an auction room where more valuable considerations
were disposed of under the speaker's hammer than in any other place on earth.'

The reaction to the scandals of the Whisky Ring and of the Crédit Mobilier pushed two reformers into the leadership of the Republicans and the Democrats in 1876; the preaching Rutherford Hayes from Grant's state of Ohio, and the reforming Tilden from New York.

Tilden won the majority of the popular vote in the election, but Republican Party finagling, with the aid of the Southern Democrats, gave the Presidency to Hayes by one vote in the Electoral College. Another civil war might have broken out at this point, when it appeared that the Republicans would even set aside the popular will to keep the White House; but Tilden acquiesced in this unjust decision. The Civil War had been so horrible that no one wanted its repetition.

Most Americans and certainly most politicians wanted peace to make themselves rich; its price was Republican withdrawal from the South and Southern acceptance of the interests of big business. The discontented West found itself isolated in front of this Southern and Eastern coalition in Congress; it had to spawn political parties of its own which tried to take Southern farmers away from their conservative Democratic leaders. But, as a Charleston

The title-page of the popular book *Sunshine and Shadow in New York (left)* which did much to reveal the more sordid aspects of urban life in the expanding city of the mid-nineteenth century. Indeed, conditions in the Northern slums almost matched those in which the Southern Negro was forced to live *(right)*.

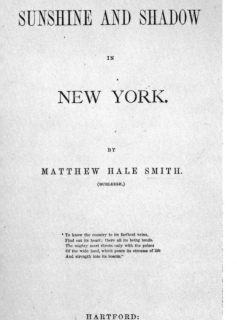

newspaper recognized in 1878, 'the permanent interests of the South lie with the East rather than with the West. The aim of the South being to . . . avoid whatever is revolutionary in politics, sociology or finance, the South must go with the East.' Thus the rationale of secession was replaced by the rationale of reunion; the consistent conservatism of the South demanded opposite policies at different times.

Economic Growth   With a permanent majority of supporters in Congress and in the Supreme Court, and with a complaisant President from the Ohio Republican dynasty usually in the White House, big business exploited and developed the United States until the end of the century. The speed of industrial growth and the energy of the entrepreneurs were incredible; their success was matched only by their ruthlessness. One of them, on reaching the Senate as a seal to his Croesus-like career, looked round the Senators and said that they represented the survival of the fittest. Jungle law and the theory of evolution applied to human behaviour were the only pretexts the great billionaires could find for their plundering of their fellow-men, who often excused such plundering in the hope that they might become billionaires as well.

The Supreme Court bowed to the political climate. With one hand it declared the Civil Rights Act unconstitutional; with the other it defended large corporations against any regulation by declaring that they had the constitutional rights of an individual. While New York and its stock market gathered in most of the liquid capital of the country and much of Europe's, lobbyists in Congress gave bribes for laws which would help the billionaires to make their fortunes in the Gilded Age. The operations of one manipulator, Jay Gould, became legendary; he would corrupt anyone for his own benefit and once declared that in Republican districts he was a Republican, in Democratic districts a Democrat, but first, last, and all the time he was for the Erie Railroad.

The monopolies and fortunes of the few grew apace. The names of Armour, Carnegie, and Rockefeller became household words for their control over aluminium, meat, steel, and oil. Yet the leading consolidators and robber barons were to be found in the railroad empires. By 1893 the United States had 170,000 miles of railroad track and four transcontinental lines; despite shoddy building, they were capitalized at nearly $10,000,000,000 and did a yearly business worth $1,200,000,000. Although there were intense slumps in 1873 and 1893, the national income of the United States grew more than six times between the outbreak of the Civil War and 1910,

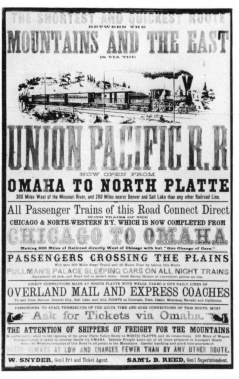

The railways provided an efficient communications network, but such was their power that all too often they ignored the public interest.

THE SCOURGE OF THE WEST.

113

Colorado, c. 1880. Until gold was discovered near Denver, in 1858, Colorado was almost a blank on the map.

while the population nearly trebled. Such an apparent cornucopia of opportunity brought in hordes of immigrants from southern and eastern as well as northern Europe. The railroads themselves could not have been built without Irish and Chinese labour, nor the steel industry without Poles and Bohemians.

While the cities swelled in pullulating slums and Chicago alone grew from a village to a city of 1,700,000 people in seventy years, the West across the Mississippi engulfed immigrants travelling in covered wagons and railroad coaches. In the twenty years after 1870, the 7,000,000 Westerners grew to 17,000,000. Tens of millions of buffalo and tens of thousands of Indians were slaughtered to make way for the settlers. Even the most inhospitable wilderness was colonized, if irrigation proved possible. Although Brigham Young and the Mormons did not found a City of Saints in Utah, they made

Sheep farmers and squatters
(*centre*) were beginning to
fence in the open prairies.
This led to the 'Sheep Wars' of
which fence-cutting (*top*)
by cattlemen (*bottom*) was one
of the least vicious aspects.

The Tabernacle in Salt Lake City, 1871 (*above*).

Harvest-time on the rich wheat farms of the northern Red River Valley (*below*).

its barrenness liveable by drudgery and faith. Farm production increased four times in value between 1860 and 1910, owing to the expansion of arable land and the help of machines.

Yet the problems of wilderness farming and isolation were terrible. The unfenced Cattle Kingdom of the Great Plains gave way to sheep and ploughs and barbed wire, not without a fight between rancher and farmer, cowboy and squatter. The extortion of Eastern lenders and railroads merely added to the bitterness caused by natural disasters. As Walter Prescott Webb, the historian of the Great Plains, noticed, the farmers there 'were far from markets, burned by drought, beaten by hail, withered by hot winds, frozen by blizzards, eaten out by the grasshoppers, exploited by capitalists, and cozened by politicians. Why should they not turn to radicalism?'

In the agricultural depressions that took place between the 1870s and the 1890s due to the overproduction of grain and the competition of the virgin wheatlands of Canada and Australia, the farmers founded their own Parties, the Greenbackers and the Grangers, which sometimes won minor elections and scared the Republicans and the Democrats. Sporadic anger in small rural towns helped the prohibitionists and the feminists to gain local victories; the closing of the saloons and votes for women came out of the West. Political discontent is good for most reform.

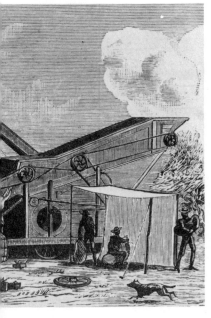

The Western farm movements failed to link up with Southern share-croppers and Eastern working-men. Although the poor whites occasionally flirted with agrarian rebels, they hated the Negro even more than they loathed the Wall Street operator, and, at a pinch, they supported the Party of their prejudices rather than their profits. The Eastern working-man, however, had begun to organize in the Knights of Labor, although he would not join the farmers since he was as interested as his employer in cheap food and expensive goods which could lead to high wages.

Labour Problems

There was an open struggle in the late nineteenth century between the private armies hired by the great industrialists and the workers striking for better conditions. Thousands lost their lives in pitched battles near the mines and factories, when scabs tried to break through picket lines or unionists were discharged for carrying a card. The Homestead and Pullman strikes were particularly bloody, and the bestial way of life inflicted on cheap immi-grant labour was exploited by the propaganda of anarchists and socialists. Yet, at a last resort, the vast mass of American workers would rather fight their bosses individually and try to make their personal fortunes than tolerate a regimented and equitable society. Trade unions and the left wing did not fare well.

The Haymarket riot, May 1886, after which four clearly innocent Anarchists were executed.

'Boss' William Marcy Tweed.

The corruption of urban politics at this time had not been equalled since the last days of Rome. Imitating the example of 'Boss' Tweed, who had made Manhattan an udder of graft, the city bosses learned how to deliver the immigrant vote in a block to the highest bidder. In return for jobs, bribes, and contracts for public works, they supported the man of their choice in their traditional Party. In the absence of all social welfare outside patronizing private charities, the urban bosses operating from their saloons did provide the only employment and aid agency in the slums. They also represented a success story to the immigrants from whose ranks they usually came. The Irish, in particular, showed a genius for urban politics and their chieftains in Tammany Hall and Boston were the pride of their downtrodden people.

Lord Bryce, the most famous commentator on the American Commonwealth after de Tocqueville, found a very different society in the New World after a gap of fifty years. He excused the city bosses by saying: 'They are the offspring of a system. Their morality is that of their surroundings. They see a door open to wealth and power, and they walk in.' The festering, jerry-built immigrant slums of the American cities gave the bosses their opportunity, and, like good Americans, they took it. To them politics was 'merely a means for getting and distributing places'.

Republican propaganda on the effects of free trade:
one of the main political issues of the 1880s.

The effects of a Tariff exclusively for Revenue as laid down in the Democratic Platform and which the Democratic Congressmen tried to enact last winter at Washington.

The effects of Protection to American Industries as guaranteed by the Republican Party and Platform.

Democratic Free-Trade Means low wages, children in rags and ignorance

Republican Protection Means good wages, happy homes and education

This view of the world, which reduced the workings of society to the organization of gain, was already endemic when the new Americans arrived. The Irish could not be blamed for out-foxing the Yankees. Yet the midden of politics stank so much that the best men avoided it and stuck to their professions. Even the Presidency went to mediocre men. 'Great men', Bryce concluded, 'have not often been chosen Presidents, first because great men are rare in politics; secondly, because the method of choice may not bring them to the top; thirdly, because they are not, in quiet times, absolutely needed.' The method of choice after the Civil War made the White House the pension scheme for Union ex-officers from the Republican Party in Ohio; and times were quiet and isolated enough to make only the well-rounded lawyer and businessman necessary.

The Ohio Dynasty

Hayes of Ohio was succeeded by Garfield of Ohio, who was assassinated in office. The only urban President of the nineteenth century, Chester Arthur, then lodged in a dead man's White House for three years, until the Democrats squeezed in with their one successful candidate between 1856 and 1912, Grover Cleveland of New York. He spent two terms in office, split by the administration of the Ohio-born Benjamin Harrison, and he was succeeded by another Ohioan, William McKinley, 'crafty with the ways that win men and hold them'. Once Virginia planter birth had made Presidents available for office, as their state straddled the borders and conflicts of North and South. Now small-town Ohio seemed to be the meeting-point between Eastern industry and Western farm, while the solid South was excluded in Democratic isolation. 'Some men have greatness thrust upon them,' the saying went, 'some are born great, and some are born in Ohio.'

James Garfield.

Besides labour troubles, the country was concerned with the veteran problem (*below left*), the position of the Negro in society (*below centre*) and the so-called 'Yellow Peril' (*below right*).

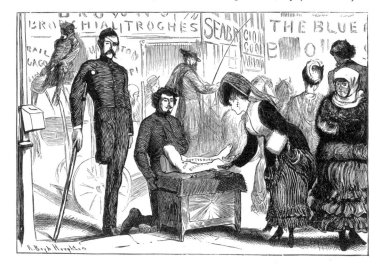

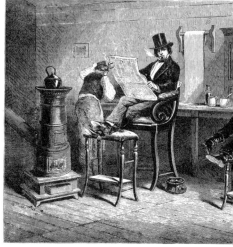

Natural gas street-lighting in Findlay, Ohio, in 1885.

J.D. Rockefeller, Sr, started the mammoth Standard Oil.

The Rockefeller residence in New York City.

While American business dragged the Presidents in its wake by the tails of their frock-coats, the Presidents did little at home or abroad to rock the boat. The Interstate Commerce Act of 1887, to regulate the railroads, and the Sherman Anti-Trust Act of 1890, to break up monopolies, were delusions and shams; they were not enforced. 'What looks like a stone-wall to a layman', Mr Dooley commented, 'is a triumphal arch to a corporation lawyer.' Federal troops were used to break strikes; federal credit and currency remained tight and geared to the gold standard; the government was vindictive towards the poor and the debtor; States' Rights were set aside by the Supreme Court in the interests of the Washington government and the corporations. The long-gone Federalists seemed to rule in both major Parties, and the dead Hamilton could smile from his coffin.

While unrestricted business made the United States the richest society in the world, its moralists and its writers preached more and more a with-drawal into the wilderness or at least into the human values of the small town or quiet suburb. In the mid-century, Hawthorne, Melville and Poe had freed American literature from the domination of British letters and had written classic works about the ambiguous results of the struggle between

American Literature

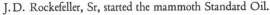

◀ Corrupt hangers-on killed Grant's hope of a third term in office.

Walt Whitman.

Henry James.

Emily Dickinson.

good and evil. Walt Whitman hymned the American virtues of labour and pioneering and democracy, their differences from the stale old world of Europe; but he, too, by the end of his life became disillusioned at the corrupt society of the Gilded Age. More and more attention was paid to the withdrawal of such as Thoreau to simplicity at Walden, or to Henry James's refugee life in Europe, or to Henry Adams's refusal to join in his hereditary business of helping to govern the nation. So crass, indeed, did the public scene appear that the greatest woman poet since Sappho, Emily Dickinson, was hardly read during her own life, because of her fear that 'publication was the auction of the Mind of Man'. The nineteenth century produced a great native American literature; but its chief quality was a wringing of the hands at the journey of the innocent and lusty Western Adam to destruction in the Babylons along the Atlantic coast.

So exuberant were the energies of the United States in the nineteenth century, so strong was the need for room for development, that the new nation took its first steps beyond its natural frontiers. Alaska had been acquired from Russia in 1867, thus outflanking the British in Canada. The colonization of the Midway Islands in the same year was the prelude to American advance into the Pacific. By the time of the annexation of Hawaii, America owned over fifty island outposts in the prairie-like seas of the Pacific, as isolated and eventually as necessary against future Japanese aggression in the Second World War as the forts of the United States Cavalry had once been against Indian attack in the Great Plains.

Thus the United States built up its strength protected by the oceans from invasion. It had solved the strains of secession at the price of exploitation of the farmer, the worker, the consumer, and the Negro. Once the worst excesses of this exploitation were checked, America could spread out beyond its shores and control half the world. The United States had shattered the first British Empire; it was to be the heir of the second. It began as the beacon of liberty and the open door for refugees from oppression; it would become the apparent defender of imperialism and reactionary governments in many countries, all to protect its own liberty.

Archibald MacLeish, born at the end of the age of isolation, was to lament bitterly the growth of America from revolutionary example to international power:

> *Freedom that was a thing to use*
> *They've made a thing to save*
> *And staked it in and fenced it round*
> *Like a dead man's grave.*
>
> *You, Thomas Jefferson,*
> *You could not lie so still,*
> *You could not bear the weight of stone*
> *On your green hill,*
>
> *You could not hold your angry tongue*
> *If you could see how bold*
> *The old stale bitter world plays new –*
> *And the new world old.*

Theodore Roosevelt.

Chapter Five

THE COMING OF REFORM

At the beginning of the twentieth century the United States was still a skein of localities which hardly knew each other. The misunderstanding between countryside and city persisted. Although the new immigrants from Europe had remained mainly in the cities, three-fifths of the 76,000,000 Americans in 1900 still lived isolated lives in villages or on farms. Dirt roads and covered wagons made slow local travel possible; but the railroads were the iron nerves of the continent, taking the hogs and grain to the cities and the goods from the factories. Where the railroad went or crossed, a town prospered and hoped to become a small city; otherwise it died. One Ohio writer noticed that his home town used to be a crossroads and was now a water-tank. The railroads were the condition of survival for rural America; this explained the venom of the country's attack on the rail companies.

The great railroads were built and controlled by tycoons, who used the device of holding companies to construct financial empires. Freight rates were too high and pushed up the prices of farm goods on the market; the farmer often received only one-sixth of the price the housewife paid in the shops. Thus more radical political movements emerged; the Populists of the 1890s took over the government of some Midwestern states and called for the use of silver to back an enlarged currency and easier credit. They even captured the conservative Democratic Party in 1896, when William Jennings Bryan declared that the East with its moneybags was 'the enemy's country'. The Populists wanted the federal government to force the railroad companies to charge fair rates, even if it meant that most un-American activity – nationali-zation. The railroads were, in fact, regulated in 1906 and briefly nationalized

'The evils of unrestricted immigration.' By 1890 New York contained twice as many Irish as Dublin, as many Germans as Hamburg, and half as many Italians as Naples.

during the First World War; but it was the later competition of heavy trucks on large highways which pushed down freight rates. As usual, a new invention rather than federal action cured an old wrong.

The radical West had other enemies to oppose besides Wall Street and Eastern capital. Fifteen million immigrants had come into the United States in the fifty years before 1900, until white Americans with parents born in America were barely half of the population. A further twelve million immigrants were to arrive in the next twenty years, mainly from Italy and central Europe. Although only two Americans in five were members of any Church, two in three of those in the cities were now Roman Catholic, while four in five Church members in the countryside were Protestants. Alien sights, alien smells, alien ways, alien faiths, alien speech had hatched ghettoes in every metropolis, while the wealth and the children of the American farmers and townsmen were themselves being sucked into the maw of urban life. The European slum seemed to have crossed the Atlantic in the steerage and to be corrupting and dominating the old American ideal.

Equality of opportunity also seemed to have been filched by the plundering of the robber barons after the Civil War. The professional classes found themselves losing political power and status to the city bosses, sustained by the slum vote and the money of the monopolists. One per cent of the population owned more than fifty per cent of the national wealth, while girls stitched away their lives in sweatshops for a few cents an hour. Democracy, the traditional safeguard of the people, had itself become corrupt. Something had to be done, if it was not already too late. As one reformer complained with considerable justification: 'The founder of the oil trust may give us back our money, but not if he send among us a hundred Wesleys can he give us back the lost ideals.'

The answer of the Populists and the Progressives, who made reform both an urban and a rural business, was more democracy. In fact, they wanted restoration more than progress. They wanted to go back to an America of small businessmen and farmers, before the days of large industries which called in illiterate immigrants to staff them. The reformers put through laws to break up the trusts, to provide for a referendum on various issues of state government, to recall bad officials, to initiate laws by popular petition, to institute a graduated income tax, to elect Senators directly, to give votes to women, to close the saloons that were the focus of corruption in the cities, and to bring hygiene to food and housing. Many of these reforms were placed in the Constitution itself, to prevent their repeal; the prohibition of the liquor trade was to have the dubious distinction of being the only constitutional amendment ever to be repealed, despite Mencken's fear that it was 'like an unpleasant fly embedded in imperishable amber'.

Populists and Progressives

Unfortunately, although the reformers succeeded in dusting off American life and politics, they did not tackle the worm at the root. There was an enduring error in American society. The Constitution had been written for an agricultural country which could afford the weakness of the federal system; it did not apply realistically to an industrial and urban system, concentrated in few hands and spread over a continent. Under a strong President, such as Theodore Roosevelt, who spent seven years in the White House after McKinley's assassination in 1901, the system of government could be made to work – but only because the Republican Party held both Houses of Congress as well as the White House. Otherwise, the checks and balances built into the Constitution proved to be merely checks on the reform of an unbalanced society.

Theodore Roosevelt

Theodore Roosevelt believed in a healthy, strong, efficient nation; he was, in George Bernard Shaw's opinion, the nearest thing to a Hohenzollern that the American Constitution allowed him to be. His measures were less against big business than bad business. He wanted things that worked well rather than virtuous ideas. Thus he tended to talk the language of the reformers and to do little about the trusts, except for a few showy cases against the more villainous companies such as Standard Oil. In fact, his fat and weak successor in the White House, William Howard Taft, prosecuted twice as many trusts in four years as Roosevelt had in seven.

Roosevelt loved to appear the man of action; but, as Mark Twain noticed, his principles looked so much like policies that they had the same 'quality of impermanency, a disposition to fade and disappear at convenience'. In the Wall Street crash of 1907, Roosevelt appealed to the greatest monopolist of all, J. P. Morgan, to halt the slide in prices; he would do little to attack the Republican golden calf of a free and unrestricted economy. A few progressive measures were passed during his administrations, but only when scandal pushed him into action. If his foreign policy was to 'speak softly and carry a big stick', his home practice was to speak loudly and carry a feather duster.

Breaker boys inside a coal breaker 1909 (*above*). The exploitation of child labour was perhaps the worst aspect of the free and unrestricted economy which favoured monopolists like J. P. Morgan (*right*).

◀ Broadway (*opposite*), showing from Cortland Street to Liberty Street, New York 1906.

Not only did the reformers fail to get a President or Congress dedicated to reform, but the very means they used to get more democracy were turned against them. The political bosses soon found how to manage publicity so well that they rendered futile the techniques of the referendum, initiative and recall, and even the primaries which some states adopted for important elections. If both major Parties were united and chose the candidates offered to the public in back rooms, what was the good of improved democracy if major Party candidates were always elected outside the rebellious Midwestern states? In despair, the reformers turned to making a third Party of their own, and the Progressive Party rose to challenge the Republicans and the Democrats.

Because of the indifferent performance of Taft in office, voters in 1912 were offered their first wide choice in a presidential election since 1860, when the Parties had splintered and Lincoln had established the Republicans in the White House. Roosevelt, thinking that Taft was presiding over the dissolution of the Republicans, tried to capture the presidential nomination at the Party convention; but Taft held patronage and the Party bosses in a tight grip and won a second nomination as the Republican leader. Roosevelt then stormed off to the Progressive Party convention and had himself chosen as the presidential hopeful of the new Party, despite the misgivings of such leading Progressives as Senator La Follette of Wisconsin who thought that Roosevelt was too much a friend of big business. The Democrats, meanwhile, had nominated the ex-President of Princeton University, the reforming Woodrow Wilson. And the Socialists had picked as their leader Eugene V. Debs, whose words sometimes made him seem as near a saint as a politician can be: 'While there is a lower class I am of it, while there is a criminal class I am of it, while there is a soul in prison I am not free.'

The four candidates set out different methods of dealing with the abuses of capitalism and industrialism. Debs wanted to end the system through nationalization; his solution polled only 1,000,000 votes out of 15,000,000, proving that old and new Americans alike were 'a society of expectant capitalists'. Taft wanted to continue the system of rule by big business and high tariffs, the traditional and successful Republican policy since the Civil War; he polled a mere 3,500,000 votes, compared with Roosevelt's 4,000,000. Roosevelt had seen that big business had come to stay, for unrestricted competition finishes with the large swallowing the small and the destruction of competition. Thus Roosevelt preached a programme of the New

President Wilson in England in 1919, just before the start of the Paris Peace Conference.

Nationalism, in which government, business, and labour would co-operate to produce an efficient and regulated America.

Roosevelt's programme was the programme of the future; but the Americans would be prepared to adopt it only in wartime. Thus the winner of the election was Woodrow Wilson, who garnered 6,000,000 votes. His solution was a return to the golden age of small businessmen and small farmers; this programme was called the New Freedom. In fact, he proved in office even stronger a President than Roosevelt had dared to be. If he talked of a return to the past, he practised the federal government of the future.

Wilson was lucky that the progressive temper of the times swept a large reform and Democratic majority into Congress at the same time that he reached the White House. Even the reactionary Supreme Court, always a block on laws for economic reform, began to give more liberal decisions, especially after Wilson's appointment to the Court of the famous progressive lawyer, Louis Brandeis – Mr Dooley had noted that the Supreme Court, although above politics in theory, always followed the election returns.

Woodrow Wilson

So Wilson, despite the checks and balances of the American political system, could be a powerful President. He turned much of the progressive programme into law. He reduced the tariff against foreign goods to three-quarters of its previous level, he regulated private banks through the Federal Reserve Board, and he gave legal protection to the rights of the 2,000,000 union members of the American Federation of Labor. A further law prevented businessmen from exploiting the work of children, even if the Supreme Court declared this mild social measure unconstitutional.

Wilson took the first few halting steps to regulate the evils of industrialism – in 1913 alone there were 1,000,000 accidents and 25,000 deaths caused by machines. Yet, as usual, improved technology and assembly-line methods and the need to conserve skilled labour were more effective in making American factories bearable places than the elementary safety regulations passed in many states. Increased efficiency and profits led to a rise in wages and improved conditions of work more than the pressure of governments or unions. American business was faced with the threat of regulation because of its failure to reform itself; but its discovery that reform led to increased output and profits because of a contented labour force actually brought in reform. Better conditions became good business, and good business was the creed of the United States.

With the beginning of the Great War in Europe in 1914, Wilson was faced with another choice between tradition and the demands of the future. Since the time of the Monroe Doctrine, the United States had little involved itself in affairs outside the Americas. Its expansion had been hidden by the fact that it had expanded across a continent almost without tenants. But with the official ending of the frontier in 1890, America's interests had pushed out more boldly across the seas. The nation had become the largest producer of food, coal, iron, and steel in the world, and this abundance of crops and goods demanded foreign markets. The contagion of imperialism, which was blocking out the world into spheres of European influence and captive markets, did not spare the United States. 'Fate has written our policy for us,' Senator Albert J. Beveridge declared, 'the trade of the world must and shall be ours.'

An engraving printed in the *Daily Graphic* in 1877.

If anything, America's case is understated because the emphasis is on light industry and agricultural produce.

If trade follows the flag, the flag also follows trade. The Spanish-American War of 1898 had left the United States with a protectorate over Cuba; the nation had also annexed the Philippines – where the Spanish empire had ended. American troops had been sent into China to help quell the Boxer Rebellion, beginning a more direct policy of intervention in the affairs of Asia than Commodore Perry's showing of the fleet to Japan. For if the east coast of America faces towards Europe and its concerns, the west coast faces towards Asia, and the south towards the Caribbean.

Roosevelt did not fail to use his big stick in the Caribbean; he annexed Puerto Rico and built a strategic canal through the puppet state of Panama. He also claimed the right to send in the marines to any Caribbean country that dared to have a revolution or to threaten American property interests. President Taft continued with this policy of 'dollar diplomacy', as did Wilson, who intervened in the internal affairs of Mexico, Nicaragua, Haiti, and the Dominican Republic. The retreat of the European powers from the Caribbean had led to the advance of the United States. Power, like nature, abhors a vacuum.

Although Amercian imperialism before the Great War seemed indefensible, it was demanded by the continuing influence of Europe on America. The struggle between Britain, Germany, and Russia for control of the world involved any other power which wished to trade. The expansion of America had made it the leading nation in terms of men and material, even if its regular army was pitiful in numbers and its navy in 1914 had only eight battleships, compared with Britain's thirty-four and Germany's twenty-one.

The fact that a massive world war was now possible for the first time in history, because of the revolution in communications, forced a firm President to evolve a policy which would protect America beyond its coasts. The strategy of the Panama Canal involved American penetration of the Caribbean as the Suez Canal demanded British penetration of Africa and the Dardanelles provoked Russia's attacks on Turkey. Given the climate of rampant nationalism and imperialism throughout the globe, American foreign policy seems notable chiefly for its restraint.

The Old World also dominated the thinking of the New. Darwin's theories of evolution continued to suit a society which was rapidly expanding and which wanted to excuse its inequalities. When John D. Rockefeller tried to justify his monopoly holdings in oil, he simply said: 'The growth of a large business is merely a survival of the fittest.' Yet the federal government

Work in progress on one of the locks of the Panama Canal, which was completed in 1914 at a cost of $366,650,000.

itself was evolving to meet the challenge of the growth of large businesses. And the theory of evolution persuaded even the Supreme Court that the holy of holies, the Constitution, might need a little alteration through interpretation, to meet the needs of new times. Change in American thought and practice became respectable for the first time since the days of the Revolution and of Reconstruction.

A more American emphasis on doing and activity replaced the Victorian preoccupation with ideals; William James's pragmatic philosophy caught this mood. Theodore Roosevelt seemed to breathe action into politics, which was to him more than the art of the possible. It was the need for the possible. 'The effort to get the impossible', he wrote, 'is always bound to be feeble.' The American economy, after all, worked better than anyone else's, although its rewards and punishments seemed to be excessive. The continent had first to be tamed and put to use before arrangements could be made for the fair allocation of its wealth.

Communications were evolving to link the separate localities. The 8000 horseless carriages of 1900 became the 3,500,000 automobiles of 1916; the numbers of newspapers doubled in this time and 21,000 cinemas already spotted the land. The aeroplane and the radio were being developed, while the spread of electric power and paved highways was stitching together the towns and the cities. The carriers of change were beginning to penetrate every backwoods hamlet.

More Americans still lived in rural than in urban areas. Although Sherwood Anderson was lamenting that 'the farmer by the stove is brother to the men of the cities, and if you listen you will find him talking as glibly and as senselessly as the best city man of us all', he lamented too soon. Commercialization of agriculture, crop specialization, business methods, new machinery, world markets, and the Sears Roebuck catalogues called 'wishing books', had done much to bind the farmer to the values of the city; but the countryside and the states still had many battles to win against the factory and the federal government.

Yet the days of isolation at home and abroad were over. Business and politics had become linked in one world. The Americas, after their period of withdrawal, had to recognize again that they were part of the globe. If the New World could never redress the balance of the Old World, it could not avoid the disturbances of its ancestral home.

138

A page from an early Sears Roebuck catalogue. The catalogue itself has been called the 'world's greatest silent salesman'.

A Ford assembly line (*above*). Henry Ford (*left*), standing next to Barney Oldfield, was the first to realize the potential of mass production.

Orville Wright at the controls of a Borden Bennett Racer in 1910. The Wright brothers' greatest service to aviation was their invention of the aileron system of control.

OVERWEIGHTED.

PRESIDENT WILSON. "HERE'S YOUR OLIVE BRANCH. NOW GET BUSY."
DOVE OF PEACE. "OF COURSE I WANT TO PLEASE EVERYBODY; BUT ISN'T THIS A BIT THICK?"

A cartoon from *Punch*, 26 March 1919.

Chapter Six

UNWILLING INVOLVEMENT

At the outbreak of the First World War, President Wilson made an official proclamation of neutrality. He urged the American people not to take sides; but they did, for most of them had roots deep in European soil. A majority supported the Allies, England, France, Italy, and Russia, because a majority were tied to these countries by family or affection; but an important minority, chiefly of the German-Americans and the Irish-Americans, supported the Central European Powers, out of love for fatherland or hatred of England which was denying independence to Ireland. The Scandinavian-Americans remained neutral, as did many Midwesterners, for the Old World seemed irrelevant in places held in the vast dish of landlocked prairies.

British strategy remained the same as it had against Napoleon, and it produced the same irritants on the United States. The policy of blockade through superior sea power denied the markets of central Europe to American businessmen; but this time the Allies offered an immense new market for American goods and war materials. While the blockade took tens of millions of dollars from the pockets of those who traded with Germany, it put billions of dollars in the pockets of the suppliers of the Allies. Thus most businessmen as well as most Americans supported the Allied cause, especially as the British played up stories of German atrocities to make the name of Hun stink in America's nose.

The huge Allied demand led to a boom in America after seven years of industrial stagnation. American factories worked full-time to meet Allied needs, American industry became tied to an Allied victory. There can be little export without involvement; once the Allies had liquidated their holdings of American stocks and shares, private banks lent vast sums to the Allies to pay for their imports from the United States. By 1917 American bankers had invested more than two billion dollars in the Allied cause.

The German answer to British surface blockade was the underwater menace. Because of American threats to enter the war if neutral ships were sunk, the Germans did not persist with their policy of unrestricted submarine warfare against all ships bound towards Allied ports. American pressure on the warring powers of Europe seemed strong enough, as the elections of 1916 approached, to protect American ships and war profits and citizens abroad without committing the decisive strength of the United States to one side or the other. Thus Wilson was able to make his slogan for re-election, 'He kept us out of war', an attractive appeal to the German-American and progressive and women's vote in the West.

Wilson just won the election by carrying the West and the South against the Republican candidate, Charles Evans Hughes, who swept the East. It was clearly a neutralist vote by the tradition-bound rural areas against the manufacturing cities, which knew that their continued boom depended on American involvement with the Allied cause. Even Senator Warren Harding from small-town Ohio, who would return American foreign policy to vacuous isolation in 1920, recognized the pull and profits of the European struggle in his keynote speech at the Republican convention, when he declared: 'The cloistered life is not possible to the potential man or the potential nation.'

Willy-nilly, because of extensive backing by Eastern industrialists, the Republican Party had to appear the war Party in 1916, just as Wilson could appear as the saviour of peace by running on his record. His narrow victory was a great personal triumph, as the Democrats had been a minority Party since the days of Grover Cleveland. His strategy of appealing to traditional attitudes made Wilson President for a second time, even if the logic of events was to lead him again to deny the hopes he had raised.

America Enters the War   Wilson took the United States into war, dreading the consequences of his decision. He feared correctly that the spirit of ruthless brutality would enter into American life. Even when the Germans had decided to gamble on a quick victory and had renewed unrestricted submarine warfare, Wilson hesitated. Only proof that the Germans were trying to incite Mexico and Japan to attack the United States and engage it in the Caribbean and the

Pacific, convinced Wilson to join the Allies. The collapse of the Russian front against the Germans made American intervention even more necessary, because the Germans could now transfer more forces to the western front. Moreover, the overthrow of the Tsarist régime in Russia by a democratic one seemed to make the issues of the war clear-cut. Four democracies, England, France, Italy, and the new Russia, were now fighting three autocracies, Germany, and the Habsburg Empire, and Turkey. America, a democracy itself, could choose only one side.

Wilson's nature, which preferred the messianic to the pragmatic, made him declare war in the name of an ideal rather than in the name of national security. He said that the reason for fighting the Central Powers was to make the world safe for peace and democracy; he did not say that America's interests would be threatened if the British fleet fell into German hands or if defeat made the Allies welsh on their debts. Although post-war events made Wilson seem a hypocrite in his declaration, perhaps no leader can take a country into war without polishing his sword with the rags of virtue.

To declare war is easier than to wage it. Despite the campaign for preparedness, the United States was unprepared in 1917. This fact, allied to the knowledge that Britain and France were drawing on their last resources to maintain their armies on the western front, had made the German government ready to risk American intervention.

The warning published by the German Embassy did little to reduce the sense of outrage felt at the sinking of the *Lusitania* in May 1915.

NOTICE!

TRAVELLERS intending to embark on the Atlantic voyage are reminded that a state of war exists between Germany and her allies and Great Britain and her allies; that the zone of war includes the waters adjacent to the British Isles; that, in accordance with formal notice given by the Imperial German Government, vessels flying the flag of Great Britain, or of any of her allies, are liable to destruction in those waters and that travellers sailing in the war zone on ships of Great Britain or her allies do so at their own risk.

IMPERIAL GERMAN EMBASSY
WASHINGTON, D. C., APRIL 22, 1915.

American soldiers with a 37 mm machine-gun in action in the Meuse-Argonne offensive of 1918.

Yet America's speed in arming and transferring her troops to the battle-fields of Europe proved decisive. Two million troops were shipped to Europe by November 1918; another 3,000,000 were training or preparing in the United States. Although short of weapons except for small arms, American armies helped to check the final German assault in 1918 and to launch the final Allied offensive that led to the Armistice. On the seas, the American fleet was large enough to make the convoy system possible; British shipping losses each month shrank to a quarter of their former total. Thus, although the Americans lost only a little over 50,000 men, while 4,000,000 Russians and Frenchmen and Britons died in action, they added the reserves necessary to win the war.

Financially, the United States shouldered its fair share of war spending, raising $33,000,000,000. Two-thirds of the total was secured by the issue of government bonds, one-third by increased taxation that made the rich and the corporations pay up to four-fifths of the immediate cost of hostilities. Meanwhile, real wages for the men in the factories and on the farms rose by a quarter between 1914 and 1918. War conditions had begun to adjust the vast difference between the wealthy and the poor in the United States – a reform that the progressives had failed to effect in peacetime.

War also brought about the federal government's intervention in business. The mass production of war materials, centralized food production and distribution, and a unified railway system were all imposed. Strikes were adjusted and labour directed. The government, indeed, supported the labour unions for the first time, so that they had 4,000,000 members by 1920. Great strides were made in heavy industry and chemicals. In fact, the war gave the United States its first proof that national planning might be the key to an equitable and expanding economy. Yet the lessons of the war were to be forgotten in peace, and the dangerous system of competitive capitalism was allowed to return. As John Maynard Keynes was to comment when America stood on the verge of the Second World War, it took preparations for war and war itself, to show America what was the true capacity of its economy and resources.

Men and supplies moving forward during the Meuse-Argonne offensive, 28 September 1918.

Whoever wins in wartime, as Brecht pointed out, the people always lose. War hysteria spread violence throughout the United States, although the nearest enemy was 3000 miles away. Not only were German-Americans attacked for little more than their origins, but radicals and dissenters were also persecuted in the name of patriotism. Debs was sentenced to ten years in prison for a speech in favour of pacifism, the only Socialist in Congress received a sentence of twenty years, and the hundred leading members of the militant Industrial Workers of the World also went to prison. In all, 1500 'political prisoners' were judged under the terms of the special and savage Espionage and Sedition and Sabotage Acts. In the war years reason and compromise seemed to be treason and cowardice. American liberties, which were being defended in Europe, were being ended at home.

The Fourteen Points The United States won the war and lost the peace. Wilson joined the Allies, rightly supposing that the security of the New World depended on the stability of the Old. He also declared that the war would be one to end all wars, and that the peace would be a 'peace without victory'. He set out Fourteen Points, asking for the right of self-determination in all European countries, the freedom of the seas, and 'a general association of nations'. There were to be no reparations, indemnities, nor humiliating peace terms to provide the seeds for future conflicts.

Yet the electorate at home ended Wilson's chances of making a bold new settlement abroad. In the elections of 1918, the American people, worried by the costs of war, sent a Republican majority back to Congress. Wilson, however, refused to include any of the Republican leaders among the peace commissioners who went with him to Versailles, although any peace treaty would need ratification by two-thirds of the Senate. He gambled on ramming the peace terms he negotiated through the Senate by appealing over its head to the people. His tactics, in his own Secretary of State's words, were those of a 'foxy ward politician'.

Wilson won most of what he wanted at Versailles. Although a myth grew up that he had been tricked there, in fact the American President was stubborn enough to force through agreement on a League of Nations, even if he had to accept an Allied indemnity against Germany and the confiscation of its colonies – the dragon's teeth of bitterness and future war. He returned to America with a majority of his countrymen probably in favour of the new League of Nations, which would police the earth and thereby prevent all future wars.

Henry Cabot Lodge.

But Wilson had called up against himself an implacable enemy, Henry Cabot Lodge, the leader of the Republicans in the Senate, always jealous of of a powerful President. Lodge prevented Wilson from securing the vote of two-thirds of the Senate to ratify the League; he was helped by Wilson's refusal to compromise with his critics. Wilson would not accept reservations which would limit America's commitment to intervene in the quarrels of the rest of the world. Moreover, Wilson's failure to control the demobiliza-tion of industry or post-war inflation led to a round of bitter strikes in 1919, which scared many Americans into thinking that another Bolshevik Revolution would break out in the United States.

Wilson further disgusted his supporters by allowing his Attorney-General to proceed on an anti-Red crusade of repression and deportation. The wave of super-patriotism called 'one hundred per cent Americanism', which flooded the country in 1919 because of war propaganda and anti-Bolshevik hysteria, washed America's mind back to its tradition of isolation. Only Wilson could, perhaps, have rolled back the tide against his League of Nations; but, in the middle of a political tour to whip up popular support for the League, he had a stroke. For his last year in the White House, only his will remained whole in his body's husk. From his sick-bed, he refused to deal with his enemies, while his Party and his policy shattered about him.

A Socialist addressing a crowd in New York in 1919.

The election of 1920 doomed the League. The Republican candidate, Warren Harding, had what Wilson called 'a bungalow mind'. His horizons were not larger than his home town or his state of Ohio. If he found himself in the White House by the largest majority given to a candidate since Monroe ran unopposed, it was because his vague wish to 'return to normalcy' coincided with the wish of a vast majority of the people. Wilson himself had won two elections by appealing to tradition; he could not blame Harding, who appealed to Jefferson's caution against entangling alliances and to a golden age before wars and the complexities of international industry and politics. 'Normalcy' may have been a time that never was; but those politicians are most successful who call on the past and act out the future.

Harding, however, both spoke and acted out the past. America did not join the League. Wilson's reason for entering the war was rendered useless. The isolation of America before 1917 was repeated after Versailles. This vacuum of power was again filled by the conflicting ambitions of the European nations and Japan. Although Hughes, now Harding's Secretary of State, called a successful conference on naval disarmament, the League was useless without the support of the most powerful nation in the world, which had originally called for the League. The New Nationalism of Theodore Roosevelt was not allowed to develop into the New Internationalism of Woodrow Wilson. By allowing itself the luxury of two decades more of isolation, the United States was to condemn itself to fight an even more bloody and destructive war.

Imbalance
of Wealth
The 1920s was a time of complacency and Republican rule. The shoddy administration of Harding was succeeded by the do-little rule of silent Calvin Coolidge, 'weaned on a pickle', and the do-much Cabinet of Herbert Hoover, who worked harder and produced more disaster than any other President. Unregulated capitalism caught the fever of a speculative boom. The war taxes on the rich were repealed, loosing huge sums for investment in the overstocked market in shares. Andrew Mellon, one of the richest industrialists in the country, remained Secretary of the Treasury throughout the decade; he believed in government of the rich by the rich for the rich. The tariff of 1922 was so high that it provoked a trade war across the world and put an end to the hopes of free trade expressed at Versailles.

The only major reform measures of the 1920s were sops to the organized farmers, who were desperate because rural income declined from nearly a

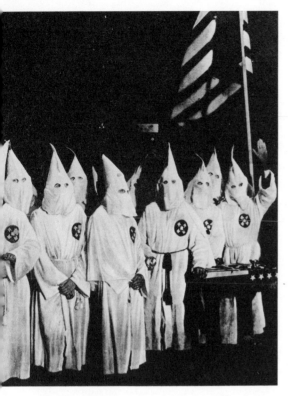

Cornelia Barns

Among the Bootleggers

"How's business, Bill?"

"Fine, fine! I've got two new mayors and a district attorney on my payroll, and two judges, a chief of police and a prohibition agent are ready to sign up next."

The law was held in disregard not only by the gangsters and bootleggers (*right*), but also, more insidiously, by the Ku Klux Klan (*left*).

quarter of the national total in 1919 to one-eighth by 1929. Farm loans and protective tariffs were granted; but Coolidge twice vetoed a bill to guarantee farm prices. The flight from the countryside to the cities became a rout; 6,000,000 more Americans left the farm for the city in the 1920s, until by 1930 only one American in four lived on a farm in what Jefferson had hoped would be a nation of small farmers. By that time, nearly one-half of Americans lived in the hundred leading cities.

The last victories of the country over the city, the crusade against the teaching of evolution, the new rise of the Ku Klux Klan to a membership of 4,000,000, the enforcement of prohibition, the laws to restrict further immigration from Europe, and the hate campaign against the Catholic and Democratic candidate for the Presidency in 1928, Alfred E. Smith, all were frenzies which provoked violence and corruption. For the United States was rushing headlong into megalopolis, and the new and lax habits of the urban rich were being scattered everywhere by the pullulating cinemas and city presses and cars and radios. Judges might denounce the Model-T Ford as 'a house of prostitution on wheels', but 1,000,000 models of the 'Tin Lizzie' were sold each year and there were 26,500,000 vehicles on the road by 1929. Indeed, the triumph of the new communications system, which was destroying the old way of life, had become necessary to keep the boom alive.

Automobiles had become the leading American industry by the end of the decade; they employed 4,000,000 men directly and indirectly. Electrical appliances, chemicals, radios, aeroplanes, the cinema, advertising, and the building trades also boomed as businesses, while only the old-fashioned industries such as shipping and textiles and coal-mining fell back. Yet, despite the falling incomes of the farmers and workers in declining industries, real wages in America continued their usual rise since the beginning of the century, until the average income of an American in 1929 was $681 a year. El Dorado seemed to have become democratic; the average American was by far the richest everyman in any nation.

Wealth, Bacon once pointed out, like muck should be well spread. Unfortunately, the vast riches of America in the 1920s were not. Too much of America's earnings was going into the hands of the few for speculation on the stock market, too little into the hands of the many to buy the goods America was producing. The average industrial share rose two-thirds in value between 1923 and 1927, then increased threefold in value by 1929. The stock market discounted not only the present and the hereafter, but also eternity, for company earnings could never keep pace with the catastrophic annual rise in share prices. A loss of confidence would cause a panic.

In addition to this imbalance at home, the prosperity of the United States depended on an unhealthy condition abroad. The First World War had turned the United States from a debtor into a creditor nation, with loans to Europe worth $13,000,000,000. America had become the keeper of the delicate balance of international payments for the first time, without understanding its new role. As it continued to export more than it imported, it could pay for its exports and the interest on its loans only by investing another $1,000,000,000 a year in Europe. As long as American investments and prosperity continued, all was well. Yet if the American investors had to call in their European loans to offset losses at home, the rug would be pulled from under world finance and trade.

F. Scott Fitzgerald.

In the 1920s, for a while,
the dream world
of the cinema (*top*),
with its glamour and
its stars like Clara Bow (*centre*),
became reality,
and people did make fortunes
overnight on the stock
market (*bottom*)
– often only to lose them
again in the Depression.

The Depression   The rug was pulled in the three years after 1929, when Wall Street's prices crashed in ruins. In those three years shares dropped to one-sixth of their previous value, imports and exports declined by two-thirds, and industrial production by a half. The European nations defaulted on their debts; England was driven off the gold standard. American farmers were reduced from subsistence to beggary; they had lost half their income in the 1920s, and now they lost another three-fifths in three years. The average income of an American dropped back to what it had been at the beginning of three decades of technological revolution. Banks failed everywhere; at least 13,000,000 workers became jobless, 1,000,000 in New York City alone. Everywhere families were evicted from their houses, for, as Mr Dooley had observed, an American's home was his castle till the mortgage fell due.

Above this mess, Herbert Hoover worked in the White House. He had been elected as 'the Great Engineer', the man who had fed the starving refugees of Belgium in the First World War and had arranged the prosperity of the 1920s as Secretary of Commerce. Now he seemed unable to feed the starving millions of America or to avert depression. Rarely has a man been elected with such confidence and produced such disappointment. The packing-case shacks of the jobless were ironically called 'Hoovervilles', trousers padded with newspapers for warmth were called 'Hoover trousers'. A mutter of discontent became a cry for change, if not revolution.

tricky dickie Nixon

Land erosion, the result of unscientific and pitifully under-capitalized farming, turned vast areas into the semi-desert of the Dust Bowl.

Hoover had been the apostle of efficient and sound American business. Yet the free economy he praised had produced world-wide disaster, and 'there is no odour', as Thoreau once wrote, 'so bad as that which arises from goodness tainted.' Hoover's measures to cope with the depression were too little, too late. Farm relief, federal loans for business, public works, all these expedients were tried half-heartedly, for they went against Hoover's grain and belief in 'rugged individualism'. Basically he believed that the Great Depression would be like all previous American slumps, a short-term affair. He declared that America had come through the fourteen previous slumps since the Civil War all right. He did not see that the total collapse of the American system of finance and of world trade would need bold federal spending and international agreements to revive the factories and the farms. He vetoed a bill to give relief and federal jobs to millions of people, because of his fear of unbalanced budgets and inflation.

The last of the three successive Presidents of the wealthy nearly presided over the liquidation of the wealthy in America. It was a time when, as Scott Fitzgerald noticed, the rich were only happy in each other's company. The rest of America had learned to hate them and their false promises. Ironically they were to be saved by the man whom they denounced as a traitor to their class, Franklin D. Roosevelt from New York, the handsome squire in a wheel-chair.

The Dust Bowl was the symbol of the Depression in the country, Hoovervilles (*left*) were its symbol in the town, and soul-destroying despair (*right*) was common to both.

Churchill and Roosevelt at Yalta in 1945.

Chapter Seven

NEW DEAL TO WORLD POWER

Any Democratic candidate could have beaten Herbert Hoover in 1932; but perhaps no other Democratic candidate could have controlled the discontent of the jobless and the farmers. Franklin Roosevelt had the best trade name for a man of action in American politics – his campaign song claimed that, as a cousin of Theodore, he was 'a chip off the block that gave us Teddy'. He added to this a genius for reassurance; when he spoke, hopes swelled out although nothing definite had been breathed. His policy was one of 'persistent, bold experimentation' to end the depression, and his trials and errors gave the people the sense that something was being done towards the promised 'new deal' for the 'forgotten man'. Harold Laski might have thought him 'a pill to cure an earthquake'; but his confidence and readiness to try almost any solution were drugs to an unnerved country. In his inaugural speech he was to say that the only thing America had to fear was fear itself; yet his own presence and voice, relayed everywhere by screen and radio, were the bromides of fear.

Franklin D. Roosevelt

The election went by a landslide to Franklin Roosevelt. Even in his home state of Iowa, Hoover was picketed by two thousand ragged men holding signs: 'In Hoover We Trusted, Now We Are Busted'. Roosevelt carried eleven of the twelve major cities that Harding had carried in 1920; he won all but six states. His huge victory, and the failure of the Socialists and the Communists to gain more than one vote in forty, showed how strongly the Americans still believed in the virtues of free enterprise, despite its colossal failure. There was no large-scale revolution in 1932, although conditions were ripe for one.

There was no revolution in 1932 because of many factors. The people trusted Roosevelt. Labour unions had conservative and weak leaders; they had lost half their membership in the 1920s. There were no organizers of the stature of Jefferson among the American radicals and no guerilla groups to form the nucleus of a rebellion. As even the conservative *Atlantic Monthly* printed:

> *It needs but one to make a star,*
> *Or light a Russian samovar.*
> *One to start a funeral pyre,*
> *One to cleanse a world by fire.*

But that one man did not come to answer the question:

> *What if our bread line should be*
> *The long slow-match of destiny?*

Although the armed farmers of the Midwest took over large areas in some states for several weeks to prevent the foreclosure of mortgages, their protest was seasonal and their militant chiefs could not hold them together. The millions of jobless grouped in the large cities were potentially more dangerous; but they had no weapons to face the small regular army, the National Guard, the State Troopers, the sheriffs, the vigilantes, the criminal gangs, and other organized or volunteer groups whose interest was in maintaining society as it was. John Steinbeck's *The Grapes of Wrath* shows how effectively small groups of armed volunteers and sheriffs attacked anyone thought to be subversive in opinion or religion or morality.

On only one occasion was the government in Washington seriously threatened. Twenty thousand veterans marched on the capital to demand the grant of a bonus from the Senate. Their leadership was, however, weak and their loyalty strong; they were easily broken up by an army detachment, led by Douglas MacArthur accompanied by Dwight Eisenhower. Although many people felt in 1932 that some form of dictatorship after the model of Mussolini's Italy might be necessary for a time, no revolution from the left found any support outside intellectual circles. Neither the right wing nor the left found a charismatic leader, and Roosevelt swept into power along the middle road, intending to give the United States not a new society but a new deal based on old ways.

The WPA was only a partial solution: it took the booming economy of war to restore full employment.

The New Deal

The first New Deal took place between 1933 and 1935. It was the programme of a dabbler in power, one ready to try anything to save capitalism. Roosevelt offered something to many people, so that most Americans could eat immediately. As the organizer of his relief programme, Harry Hopkins, said: 'Hunger is not debatable.' Roosevelt also did not find debatable the fitness of an economic system which had collapsed so disastrously. He acted at once to salvage both private property and people, both banks and human bellies; but he remained conservative at the roots.

He first saved the private banks by lending them $1,000,000,000 quickly; many people had expected he would nationalize them instead. Although banking and stock market laws now prevented the abuses which had allowed the fevered boom before 1929, banks and shares were left in the hands of the old abusers. Roosevelt was merely shoring up a shattered system, patching instead of reconstructing. Moreover, no public housing projects were begun; $6,000,000,000 more went into the moribund building industry and loans to home-owners threatened with eviction because of their debts.

Mrs Frances D. Perkins, Secretary of Labor.

Codes of fair practice were written for the big unions and the big employers; the consequence was that small businessmen along with the unskilled and unorganized workers found themselves squeezed even more between the giant organizations of businessmen and skilled workers. For 200 large corporations now owned nearly half the non-financial assets of American industry, and these mammoths were protected from anti-trust laws by Roosevelt in order to get the machines in the factories turning again.

Yet, true to his promise, Roosevelt did not forget the forgotten man. Some 4,000,000 people were put to work on various projects, chiefly improving the National Parks and highways of the country. Here Franklin Roosevelt showed himself a true disciple of Theodore, who had always stressed the need for the conservation of America's natural beauty and resources. The farmers, meanwhile, were paid for ploughing under their surplus crops in order to drive up prices; through a combination of loans and luck, they doubled their income between 1933 and 1935. Roosevelt had at last recognized the fact that the American farmers, who grew such a vast surplus of cheap food for the cities by their efficiency, should be subsidized by taxes collected from the cities. That principle has been upheld ever since.

Yet these steps were little more than an inferior version of Wilson's policies in the First World War. Small businessmen, poor farmers, and aged people had hardly been helped. Roosevelt was pushed towards more radical remedies and the economic theories of Keynes by the rise of demagogues such as Huey Long, the Kingfish of Louisiana, and Father Coughlin, the radio priest, who were gaining mass support by their proposals to expropriate the rich and share out their wealth. He feared semi-Fascist uprisings in support of Long and Coughlin by the 10,500,000 people still jobless in 1935. Keynes's theory of deficit spending and his cunning graft of socialism on to capitalism, to modify both doctrines, was preferred to the drastic theories of Marxism or Fascism. Once again, the moderate theories of the Old World were called in to redress the balance of the New.

Keynes wanted the government to borrow on the future in time of slump and to put money into the pockets of the people, so that they could consume enough goods to get the factories moving again. From this concept grew the idea of the Gross National Product, a theory which allowed the United States to mobilize its resources much more effectively than the Axis Powers in the Second World War. Although the declaration of war was needed to make the American government adopt the more rigorous parts of Keynesian economics, some of his theories had already become incorporated in the second New Deal.

Roosevelt first tried to put money in the pockets of the jobless through the *WPA* Works Progress Administration. Some 3,000,000 people were regularly employed and more than $11,000,000,000 spent in its first six years; even artists and writers and musicians were for the first time hired by the govern‚ ment. Roosevelt also decided to take an important step in the direction of the Welfare State; a Social Security Act provided insurance against sickness and old age for 28,000,000 American workers. The power of the labour unions against employers and the courts was further strengthened by the Wagner Act, while an impartial National Labor Relations Board was set up to be a referee in time of strikes. Public housing projects were started, and federal schemes to bring electricity to the countryside. New government commissions went about regulating big business, for Roosevelt had seen that big business would not reform itself. Its aims were always more profits, not more jobs.

The Government set up work camps for the unemployed (*left*), but this did not get to the root of the bitter conflict between labour and management (*right*).

Thus, before the election of 1936, Roosevelt openly declared himself on the side of the 'one-third of a nation ill-housed, ill-clad, ill-nourished'. He had won the greatest mass following enjoyed by any President since the days of Andrew Jackson; his Republican critics said he had done so by making the government 'a milch cow with 125,000,000 teats'. Yet it was the Republicans who had offered the people circuses in the 1920s; the Democrats now only offered bread. As a result, Roosevelt won a second term by a landslide, carrying the whole United States except for Maine and Vermont.

This huge mandate made him feel stronger in office, ready to attack even the holiest of American institutions – the Supreme Court. But his attempt to pack the backward-looking Court failed, and, with the onset of a recession in 1937, Roosevelt began to revise his policies. A third New Deal began, suspiciously like Woodrow Wilson's New Freedom, with Roosevelt backing individual liberty and state and local power. It took the Second World War and a jolt into international responsibility to move Roosevelt back to the paths of the second New Deal. The pre-war years represented both over-confidence and a failure in Roosevelt's nerve. He seemed to vacillate between the abuse and the fear of power.

Although Roosevelt failed to alter the composition of the Supreme Court, it now stopped declaring Roosevelt's laws unconstitutional and began giving progressive judgements that steadily changed it from the imp of reaction to the apostle of reform. The fortunate deaths of some old Justices allowed Roosevelt to appoint new ones, ready to accept change. The Supreme Court began to push for progress, gradually taking on the character that would eventually make it the supporter of Civil Rights for the Negro and of fair representation for urban dwellers in the state legislatures.

Made more cautious by failure, Roosevelt became sensitive to charges of collectivism and 'supergovernment'. He stopped direct federal intervention and channelled loans through local authorities – despite the success of such
TVA huge government projects as the Tennessee Valley Authority, which began the control and use of the tantrums of the Mississippi River. Perhaps nothing illustrated Roosevelt's retreat from ideas of large-scale business and government better than his idea to start busting the trusts again. After failing to co-operate with or regulate big business, Roosevelt now sought to split it up in the interests of cheap goods for the consumer. A determined attack was launched on price-fixing. The originator of the New Deals now confessed how old-fashioned the last of them was. 'As a Nation we have

Part of the massive T V A project. ▶

Clifford Odets.

John Dos Passos.

rejected any radical revolutionary programme', he declared in 1938. 'For a permanent correction of grave weaknesses in our economic system we have relied on new applications of old democratic processes.'

Roosevelt had saved the old system with the New Deals. He had prevented any right-wing dictatorship from coming into power; the two leading figures of the mid-1930s, Long and Coughlin, rose too late to challenge the President. Yet economic change in the depression profoundly altered society. Despite appeals to get back to the land, the drift to the cities was not reversed. Where there had been three tractors in 1930 there were five by 1940, and only two jobs for every five migrant farm workers. The result of this mechanization and surplus of rural labour was the growth of the city slums.

Moreover, even the New Deals could not distribute wealth fairly about the nation. The South, where more than one in five Americans lived, received less than one-tenth of the national income. Despite the temporary success of relief and the long-term success of welfare projects, the New Deals were perhaps most powerful in lifting the morale of the people – particularly of the intellectuals. Those who had been disgusted with the materialist spree of the 1920s liked the idealism in action of the 1930s. Dos Passos and Farrell and Steinbeck injected social criticism into the carcass of the American novel, flabby since the early days of Dreiser; Odets and Rice did the same for the American stage. Though none of the social writers was to touch the greatness of a Faulkner or an O'Neill, they made their talents as significant as possible in the wastelands short of genius.

In his early days as President, Roosevelt was as much of an isolationist as Harding. Hoover had seen that the way out of the Depression was a revival of international trade; but Roosevelt had put an end to international negotiations and had tried for a nationalist solution. The continuing breakdown of world trade played into the hands of the Nazis in Germany, who capitalized on social chaos to put over their own version of economic nationalism. Although Roosevelt's Secretary of State negotiated a series of trade agreements with no less than twenty-one separate nations by 1940, American commerce during the 1930s only reached half its volume during the 1920s.

Roosevelt's political isolationism matched his programme of economic self-sufficiency. He adopted a 'Good Neighbor' policy in the Caribbean and gave up the doctrine of the 'right of intervention' in the revolutions of other nations in the Americas. He withdrew the marines from Cuba, Haiti,

Eugene O'Neill.

William Faulkner.

John Steinbeck.

163

Panama, and the Dominican Republic. Even the expropriation of American oil interests in Mexico did not provoke armed intervention.

In distant foreign affairs Roosevelt was equally concerned with a policy of peace at any price. Japan's conquest of Manchuria did not provoke him to intervene on behalf of the hard-pressed Chinese. Neither did he try a firm policy towards Hitler or Mussolini, beyond one speech asking to 'quarantine the aggressors' in co-operation with the League of Nations. He could go no further than this pious hope, because polls showed that most of Congress and two-thirds of the American people supported neutrality. Roosevelt's one act of courage was to recognize Soviet Russia, diplomatically invisible to the United States since the Bolshevik Revolution.

Congress once again displayed the same mixture of isolationism and militancy that was hardly puzzling in a nation set apart by geography yet conscious of its own strength. A billion dollars was voted for the construction of new warships, enough to sink the combined fleets of Japan, Germany, and Italy. With the Russo-German Pact and the crises of 1939, Roosevelt asked for an increase in the defence budget. 'We, no more than other nations,' he wrote to Congress, 'can afford to be surrounded by the enemies of our faith and our humanity.' Although various neutralist laws still hampered Roosevelt from aiding the European democracies, he had himself recognized that American security did depend on the peace of Europe and Asia, as well as on that of the Americas.

The isolation of the United States in the 1920s and 1930s had made it necessary for Roosevelt to face again Wilson's situation after 1914. America's refusal to play the part of a world power had allowed lesser powers to fill the vacuum. Meanwhile, modern invention had made war global, not local. American institutions could not be defended now within the frontiers of the Monroe Doctrine.

When Hitler attacked Poland in 1939, and Britain and France went to war against Germany, the majority of the American people again supported the democratic powers. Yet their support was merely emotional; polls showed that most of them wanted an Allied victory without American intervention. As long as the traditional guarantor of the Monroe Doctrine, the British fleet, was still afloat, the United States could feel safe. Yet, as Roosevelt warned, 'even a neutral has a right to take account of facts.'

The facts were even more simple than in 1914, that Germany was the authoritarian aggressor and that the Allied market could support an American boom. The neutrality laws were repealed and the Allies were allowed to buy goods, if they could pay for them in dollars and ship them away. American ships were forbidden to enter certain war zones, since Roosevelt did not want a repetition of the sinkings that had provoked Wilson so sorely.

The fall of France, the entry of Italy into the war, and the blitz of London led to a change in American opinion and policy. Britain was left as the last defender of democracy and its defeat seemed likely; Joseph Kennedy, the American ambassador in London, forecast this defeat. War materials *Lend-Lease* were now sold or bartered to Britain, including fifty old destroyers in return for bases in Newfoundland and the Caribbean to protect America's coasts. Roosevelt excused this violation of the policy of neutrality by saying that his action was the most important in reinforcement of national defence since Thomas Jefferson bought Louisiana from Napoleon.

The President did not, however, confirm this deal until he had won a third term in the White House. No man had ever served three terms before. When Coolidge had seemed to seek a third term in 1928, the Senate had passed a resolution that departure from the tradition, set by George Washington, of serving two terms only would be 'unwise, unpatriotic, and fraught with peril to our free institutions'. Yet it was because the free institutions of the United States were in peril that Roosevelt asked his Party to nominate him for a third term. Only after his death was an amendment to the Constitution passed preventing any future President from being elected more than twice.

On his return to America Joseph P. Kennedy, the United States ambassador to London, declined to make an official statement on the European situation until he had seen the President.

Wendell Willkie.

The Republicans nominated as their presidential candidate the internationalist Wendell Willkie, who was to die known for his humble origins and his book, *One World*. He was a formidable candidate, even if connections with big business gave him the name of 'just a simple, barefoot Wall Street lawyer'. His accusations that Roosevelt was warmongering provoked an emphatic promise of peace from Roosevelt. 'Your boys are not going to be sent into any foreign wars', he assured the mothers and fathers of America. 'The purpose of our defence is defence.' Yet Willkie hit harder with claims that Roosevelt was setting up a dictatorship and that the New Deals had distributed poverty rather than wealth. Luckily for Roosevelt, the supply of war materials to the Allies had brought the number of unemployed down to 8,000,000; mobilization was to provide the answer to the barrenness of peace.

Roosevelt won the election only by 4,000,000 votes; he lost ten states to Willkie who brought the German-Americans of the Midwest back into the Republican fold. Once safe in the White House again, Roosevelt declared that America would become the 'arsenal of democracy' and send more aid to Britain. By the Lend-Lease Act of March 1941, $7,000,000,000 was lent to Britain to buy war materials in the United States. The result was that unemployment dropped by 2,500,000 as the factories began surging into

Pearl Harbor, 7 December 1941. The photograph shows the battleship *Arizona*.

production. Moreover, American destroyers went into action against German submarines in the Atlantic, and Roosevelt and Churchill issued the Atlantic Charter, a declaration of post-war hopes similar to Wilson's Fourteen Points, but asking for more economic justice.

When Germany invaded Russia, another $6,000,000,000 of Lend-Lease went to Stalin. Yet Britain was unable to get the United States to prepare for a possible attack by Japan in the Far East. Now that Hitler had engaged Russia on her western front, Japan was freed from the fear of a Russian attack through Manchuria. The weakness of the democracies in the Pacific was a temptation to assault their possessions there. Roosevelt's embargo on the export of iron, steel, and oil to Japan, in order to prevent its total victory over China, proved merely an irritant rather than a deterrent, as did his insistence that Japan should withdraw from China and Indo-China before a peace settlement could be negotiated to cover the whole Pacific. Instead, Japan decided to ally itself with Germany and Italy. On 7 December 1941, the *Pearl Harbor* Japanese struck at the great American military base of Pearl Harbor in Hawaii. They inflicted on the United States the most humiliating defeat in its history. Soon afterwards, Japanese armies overran the Philippines, Malaya, Hong Kong, and other American and British bases.

The United States 151st Infantry Division advancing during bitter fighting on Carabao in the Philippines, April 1945.

Congress immediately declared war on Japan. It was not necessary to do so on Germany and Italy, for both declared war on the United States a few days later. McKinley's assertion at the beginning of the century, 'The period of exclusiveness is past', at last became the reality of American foreign policy. The country that had repudiated the League of Nations at the end of the First World War was to set up the headquarters of the United Nations in New York at the end of the Second.

Normandy,
June 1944.

The American armed forces put an end to unemployment; by 1945
more than 12,000,000 Americans were serving in uniform. The losses of this
vast army were small compared with the many millions lost by the Russian
forces – only 290,000 combatants killed and 670,000 wounded. Rationing
was not severe, and there was no bombing of American cities. Geographical
isolation and relative abundance pushed the reality of war far from the
homeland.

A storage depot, England 1944. By June there were twenty-one American divisions in the United Kingdom.

Yet the mobilization of production was great and effective. The war stimulated industrial activity and invention among the Allies to an astonishing level. The problem of detecting the enemy produced radar and stimulated electronic development. The problem of curing wounds led to the widespread use of penicillin and blood-plasma techniques. The problem of killing insects around army camps produced DDT and other pesticides. And the problem of killing other men produced heavier and heavier tanks and guns and ships and mines and shells and fuses, and finally produced the atomic bomb. The full consequences of that last production have yet to become apparent.

Despite various expedients to avoid Wilson's centralized planning during the First World War, Roosevelt had to adopt his methods to deal with the Second. Planned enterprise freed the capacity of American industry. In the six years after 1939, industrial production doubled, while agricultural production rose by one-fifth and farmers' incomes four times over. At last the rural standard of living matched the urban. By the end of the war in Europe, American factories were producing twice as many war goods as Germany, Italy, and Japan put together. American output swamped the Axis attack.

The war cost ten times as much as the First World War and double the amount spent in all American history before its outbreak. Two-fifths of the cost came from increased taxes on the rich and on corporations, the rest from the national debt which increased six times. Mellon's idea in the 1920s, that the national debt could be paid off, now seemed as much of a dream as the idea that booms could be almost permanent – except during a permanent state of war. Real wages rose in the war years by one-third, and the Negroes of the South were liberated from their slavery to the land by serving at good wages in the armed forces or in Northern factories. Union membership rose to 15,000,000 and American workers and farmers reached an undreamt-of level of prosperity.

Even war hysteria was not excessive. Only the 112,000 Japanese-Americans lost their property and were herded into camps. The German-Americans were no longer hounded. The nation seemed now to accept the Hun Peril at home; but it could not yet accept the Yellow Peril, nor the Black Peril from the Negroes moving out of peonage in the South to the opportunity of the industrial cities.

In June 1941 Roosevelt established the Committee on Fair Employment Practice and prohibited racial discrimination in government, the armed forces *(below)* and the defence industries. This in effect prepared the way for the Civil Rights programme.

The strategy of the war overseas often depended on diplomacy rather than military needs. The first priority of the United States was its own defence. Roosevelt therefore pursued the war in the Pacific with energy. Secondly, he had to choose between the military demands of Britain, Russia, and the Free French. He preferred the claims of Churchill, thus embittering Stalin and de Gaulle. The war years were ones of extraordinary personal contact; Roosevelt and Churchill met eight times. At these meetings Churchill persuaded Roosevelt to back the British strategy of opening a 'Second Front' through Italy rather than France to take pressure off the Russians, for he did not want central Europe to fall into the hands of the Russian armies, which were steadily pushing back the Germans after the victory of Stalingrad.

While the war in Europe was largely a British affair until the landing in France in 1944, the brunt of the war in the Pacific fell on the Americans. They fought the Japanese bitterly from archipelago to island; the Japanese thrust towards Australia was first contained and then repulsed. Roosevelt could ask for a fourth term in office, with victory all but won. 'As a good soldier', he said he would serve another term to finish off the war. But his health was known to be weak and a great struggle developed over the Vice-Presidency, 'Your Superfluous Excellency', whose role was to wait for a dead man's shoes. Senator Harry S. Truman, a little-known machine politician from Missouri, as tough as a cottonwood root, won the struggle.

The Republicans named Thomas E. Dewey, the Governor of New York, as their candidate. His mind was able; but his moustache gave him the look of the city slicker. He ran a good campaign against Roosevelt, claiming correctly that 'it took a war to make jobs under the New Deal'. He could not, however, attack Roosevelt's handling of the war without seeming unpatriotic, and Roosevelt campaigned on his success overseas, hardly mentioning domestic affairs. When things go well abroad, the President is strengthened at home. So Roosevelt won again by 3,600,000 votes, losing a little more strength to the Republicans.

Wilson's example proved a terrible warning to Roosevelt. He went out of his way to woo the Republican leader of the isolationists, Senator Vandenberg. In a remarkable switch, Vandenberg rejected the 'old way' which had twice taken America 'to Europe's interminable battlefields within a quarter of a century'. Thus Roosevelt could go to his final conference with Churchill and Stalin at Yalta and redraw the post-war map of the world, secure in the knowledge that the Senate would probably ratify the peace.

General Eisenhower, the supreme allied commander, briefing paratroops before D-Day, 6 June 1944.

At Yalta the geography of the cold war was largely settled. Germany was *Yalta* divided and the principle of the United Nations accepted. Although Stalin agreed that the countries of eastern Europe should be allowed to decide their future by free and democratic elections, he knew well that Communist governments would rule behind the line along which the Red Army stopped. Neither Roosevelt nor Churchill could afford to plunge their war-weary countries into another war against their Russian ally, if its dictator insisted on imposing his solution on the countries he occupied.

Roosevelt's failure was less one of diplomacy than of strategy. He refused to break the Yalta agreement, even when Stalin had imposed Communist governments on Poland and Rumania: Churchill's plan to push forward the Allied armies to meet the Red Army as far east as Berlin or Prague was shelved. Here Roosevelt was badly advised by his commander-in-chief in Europe, General Dwight Eisenhower, who believed in the myth of a German redoubt in Bavaria and refused to expose the Allied flank by a swift advance across the German plain. Before Roosevelt had time to reconsider, he was dead. Harry Truman, new in office, took Eisenhower's advice. Thus Russian armies occupied Berlin and Prague first, the Nazi government surrendered unconditionally, and the present line of cold war in Europe was established. The patterns of new societies, Communist and capitalist, grew up behind the forward trenches of the armies sent out by the differing economies.

In the Pacific the tactics that had defeated Hitler were used against the Japanese. Mass invasion from the sea took island after island, while heavy bombing raids destroyed two-fifths of the houses in Japan and broke civilian morale. Unlike that of Germany, Japan's industry was shattered by air strikes. Finally, atomic bombs were dropped on Hiroshima and Nagasaki, after the Japanese Cabinet had rejected an ultimatum which threatened the country with 'utter devastation'. Russia also entered the war against Japan at the last moment, in order to share in the spoils. And so the Atomic Age began, with a Western power imposing its will on an Eastern by nuclear force.

Bikini Atoll, 25 July 1946. This underwater test was carried out almost a year after the horrors of Hiroshima and Nagasaki.

Chapter Eight

THE ROAD TO THE GREAT SOCIETY

Truman proved more able in power than anyone had suspected. He used *The Fair Deal* Roosevelt's methods of persuasion and he accepted the responsibility of his office. The Presidency, he said, was 'where the buck stopped'. He also learnt from Wilson's mistakes at home after the First World War and decided to mobilize for peace. He aimed to complete the New Deal by a Fair Deal. The switching, by the 'G.I. Bill of Rights', of more than ten million Americans from the armed forces back to civilian jobs was helped through loans and services and education for veterans. The Employment Act of 1946 officially accepted federal responsibility for keeping up a high level of employment by priming the economy when necessary; but, even so, Truman sold back the one-fifth of private industry taken over by the government during the war. Truman's Fair Deal did not include any nationalization. Like every other President, Truman put private ownership first after God.

Truman also rearranged the workings of government. A National Security Act gave a single Secretary of Defence power over the Joint Chiefs of Staff and set up the National Security Council and the notorious Central Intelligence Agency, which would perpetuate the spy service born in the war. Further measures streamlined the bureaucracy. Yet Truman failed with more ambitious measures to extend social security and increase the minimum wage, for the Republicans won control of both Houses of Congress in 1946 and were determined on obstruction after their fourteen years in the wilderness.

The new conservative temper of the nation's lawmakers, 'the worst Congress in history' in Truman's opinion, was shown by the passage of the

◀ The Secretariat and the General Assembly (foreground) of the United Nations in New York.

Taft-Hartley Act, which forbade closed shops and the militant strike tactics used in the late 1930s by the new group of mass unions, the Congress of Industrial Organizations. Taxes were reduced for the benefit of the rich; public housing projects were thrown out. The Fair Deal was trumped – except in the field of farming, where the Republicans hoped to pile up new votes. Flexible government support of farm prices was indefinitely continued, because the Corn Belt was expected to decide the next election.

It did. The result was the most unexpected one in any American election. For the first time in their Party's history, the Republicans nominated their defeated candidate, Dewey, despite the celebrated remark: 'How can you expect a soufflé to rise twice?' Both the Dixiecrat right and the Progressive left split off from the Democrats, taking four Southern states out of the Democratic column and throwing three Northern states, including New York, to the Republicans because of the Progressive garnering of Democratic votes. Truman seemed bound to emulate Taft's disaster in 1912 when his Party had split. Yet he fought a gutsy campaign and squeaked home on the votes of the Midwest and the Far West, while Dewey, who had expected to coast home on his urban vote, snatched defeat from the jaws of victory.

The Democrats also snatched back control of both Houses of Congress. Thus Truman, victor in his own right rather than by inheritance, was able to push through measures increasing social security, nearly doubling the minimum wage, continuing rent control, giving federal funds for slum clearance and rehousing, and building more dams and power stations. His programme for national health insurance, however, failed because of the savage opposition of the organized American doctors, while his programme for federal aid to schools was blocked by the Roman Catholics' demand for similar aid to parochial schools. Truman's need of the Southern bloc's votes in the Senate also prevented any advance on Civil Rights. The Negroes, who had served so well in war, made little progress in peace.

In foreign policy, however, a revolution took place. The charter of the *United Nations* United Nations was chiefly an American document. The Declaration of Independence was now replaced by a declaration of interdependence, America's first formal admission that it lived with other nations in one world. With the setting up of the General Assembly and the Security Council and the Secretariat of the United Nations in Manhattan, the American people were faced with the physical reminder that most of the nations of the world had now slipped under their umbrella of isolation.

179

◀ The Grand Coulee dam.

President Truman with ex-President Hoover who, in 1947, was elected chairman of a commission on the organization of the executive branch of the government.

Robert Schuman, the French Minister of Foreign Affairs, speaking at the third anniversary of the Economic Co-operation Administration in 1951.

This cartoon from the *New York Herald-Tribune* was one of the more outspoken criticisms of the Senator from Wisconsin.

Right in Front of the McCarthy Fan Club

The Monroe Doctrine was replaced by the Truman Doctrine, which led to the rebuilding of Europe on American money and the containment of Communism across the globe by aid and arms. If the British fleet had once protected the Americas, the inadequacy of that fleet now led the United States to take over Britain's imperial role. American power replaced British influence in Turkey, Greece, Iran, and China, until the victory of Mao Tse-tung over Chiang Kai-shek brought over the biggest nation of all to Communism.

Europe was preserved for capitalism by the injection of $12,000,000,000 before 1951 and by the creation of the North Atlantic Treaty Organization to provide for a common defence. But Communist successes in China and eastern Europe made America's suspicion of Russia grow into fear. This fear swelled into hysteria at home, where Truman was forced to purge the

Joseph McCarthy.

Civil Service of many suspected sympathizers with Russia and Senator McCarthy blew up like a ten days' corpse on the gas of suspicion and Red-baiting. The discovery that certain people in America and Canada and Britain had passed atomic secrets to the Russians, who could now explode nuclear weapons of their own, returned most people to the rabid mania for persecution that rises and declines regularly in American life. Employers sacked and black-listed employees merely accused of Communism. Guilt was established by smear, loss of job followed on false witness. The weak American Communist Party was soon policed out of significance. Until the rapid decline of Senator McCarthy, the American people had little to fear from Communism at home except the fear of Communism itself.

Abroad, however, the United States became involved in the Korean War. The North Korean régime had not thought that the Americans would consider South Korea necessary for the defence of the Pacific, so it was caught by surprise when Truman ordered the American army and navy to help the defeated South Koreans. The lucky absence of Russia from the Security Council had allowed America's intervention in Korea as a member of the United Nations, since the North Koreans were condemned as aggressors.

General MacArthur (centre) with Lieutenant-General Walker (right). Korea, August 1950.

Eisenhower, the President-elect, inspecting South Korean troops in Korea, 1952.

The war itself stimulated the flagging economy of America, and, despite a see-saw campaign and massive Chinese intervention, the fighting resulted in a stalemate roughly along the line of the old borders of South Korea. General MacArthur, in charge of the forces of the United Nations, tried to persuade Truman to blockade China and use atomic bombs against its cities. When Truman ignored his advice for fear of provoking a third World War, MacArthur wrote to Republicans in Congress that an open conflict with China was necessary. 'By this act', Truman later wrote, 'MacArthur left me no choice – I could no longer tolerate his insubordination.' So Truman dismissed him, confirming in the most dramatic manner that civil power still ruled military power in the United States.

MacArthur was cheered all the way into retirement and insignificance. The general who profited from Truman's bold act was Eisenhower. 'There is no substitute for victory', MacArthur had declared; but he had been stalemated in Korea. The Republicans might use MacArthur as a stick to beat the Democrats; but they wanted Eisenhower, who had never lost a military campaign, to ride home in the presidential campaign of 1952. After the winning example of Washington and Jackson and Zachary Taylor and Grant, Eisenhower was the one man in the United States almost

Dwight D. Eisenhower

183

John Foster Dulles, Churchill, Eisenhower and Eden on the lawn of the White House.

certain to succeed to the White House – traditionally the pension scheme for victors of major wars.

Against Eisenhower the Democrats ran a witty liberal intellectual, Adlai Stevenson, the Governor of Illinois. A man of passionate integrity, he fought a loser's campaign. While Eisenhower's speeches made him seem 'pretty much for mother, home, and heaven', Stevenson's made him seem pretty much for education rather than the Presidency. 'Better we lose the election', he declared, 'than mislead the people; and better we lose than mis-govern the people.' He refused to defend Truman's record, which had become tarred by the inflation and corruption and discontent resulting from the Korean War. When Eisenhower made much of the peace theme that normally wins American elections, saying that he himself would 'go to Korea' to seek 'an early and honourable' end to the war, he seemed to offer exactly the right blend of iron fist and velvet glove to an electorate that blamed the Democrats for being too soft on Communism at home and too hard overseas.

The election of 1952 gave the White House to the Republicans by 6,500,000 votes, although they only tied in the Senate and barely won in the House of Representatives. The Democrats, even in their dog days, still held on to nearly half of the American voters. Eisenhower's victory was personal rather than political; Americans voted for him with all the confidence that they would feel in a favourite uncle.

184

Eisenhower did, indeed, bring peace in Korea, although the huge waste of money and men gained no ground from the Communists. Yet one thing was proved there, that a limited war in the Atomic Age need not spread into a world war. After this keeping of his promise, Eisenhower delegated foreign policy to his Secretary of State, the stern John Foster Dulles. In fact, Eisenhower's whole method of administration consisted in letting the buck stop in each Cabinet office. He wished to be above politics and to appeal to all men. He would not plunge himself into the difficulty of daily decision and personal responsibility. He failed to dominate politics, and, by choosing to appear a good man, he became a bad President, the mere figurehead of the business forces which had filled his campaign chest. *John Foster Dulles*

Eisenhower meant to balance the budget once he was in office; but he found even that beyond his great powers of equilibrium. Although no reformist, he had to continue a modified version of the Fair Deal through the 1950s to sustain the appeal of the Republican Party in the cities. After the end of the Korean War had led to a slump, Eisenhower had to accept the principle of federal spending. Government money continued to pour into foreign aid, American welfare, and farms. Yet little new thinking was done, because four years of boom succeeded the slump of 1953; the Gross National Product rose by one-sixth in these years. The New Deal had become traditional and its continuation seemed just fine and almost natural.

Adlai Stevenson in West Berlin. Behind him is the Berlin Wall.

Abroad Dulles played a strong hand, walking on the edge of war. His policy of firm opposition to Communist expansion was called brinkmanship; but it was little more than Truman's policy of containment. He did not begin another Korea in Indo-China in support of the French; he did not send help to the rebels in East Germany in 1953 nor in Hungary in 1956. He spoke loudly and carried the big atomic stick in American air bases girdling Russia; but the stick was never used in a preventive war, although America's early nuclear strength was far superior to Russia's. The South-East Asia Treaty Organization was set up to contain China in the same way as NATO had been set up to contain Russia. And so Eisenhower could go to the country again in 1956 with the genuine slogan of 'peace, progress, prosperity'.

He won a second term easily against the same opponent, despite Stevenson's fair comment that the Republicans coveted Eisenhower as a candidate and ignored him as a leader. The Hungarian revolution and the Suez crisis played into Eisenhower's hand, because few want to change captains when the boat is rocking. America's consistent denunciation of both British and French imperialism in Egypt and of Russian imperialism in Hungary restored it to its revolutionary posture as the terror of the colonial powers.

Thus Eisenhower rode back into Washington with an increased majority, although he had already had one heart attack and was not expected to survive another four years in office. A vote for Eisenhower might well have meant a vote for the Vice-President, Richard Nixon, an aggressive politician from California, so evasive that he was accused of being the only man able to campaign in Scylla and Charybdis and carry both precincts.

Eisenhower's victory, however, was matched by Party defeat. Americans seemed to prefer Eisenhower nationally and Democrats locally. The trouble with a man who sets himself above politics is that he does not help those who stay within politics. Eisenhower had little help from Congress during his second term, except over conservative or military measures. Then the Republicans could get support from Southern Democrats at the price of doing nothing about Civil Rights. The only important change in American policy was military; the conventional army was lopped and a nuclear arsenal built up. The launching of the first Russian sputnik was a severe blow and money was poured into research to bridge the mythical 'missile gap'. American opinion veered against Eisenhower; the man who had won the Second World War seemed to be losing the cold war.

Khrushchev and Castro attending the fifteenth general assembly of the United Nations in New York, September 1960.

A succession of failures in foreign policy also hit at Eisenhower. There *Cuba* were misadventures in the Middle East and disaster in Cuba, where the Marxist régime of Fidel Castro replaced a reactionary dictatorship. Eisenhower seemed so weak that he could not even prevent Communism from establishing itself ninety miles off the shores of the United States. The Congressional elections of 1958 gave the Democrats nearly as many seats as they had held during the New Deals. Despite the death of Dulles and Eisenhower's personal handling of foreign politics, the disastrous incident of the U-2 spy plane shot down over Russia put an end to any hopes of a thaw in the cold war.

Stagnation seemed to have reached America; its image was the ailing old general in the White House. Marxism had come to the New World, the growth rate of America's economy had begun to sink to half that of Russia and Europe, and automation had made the unemployment figures stick at the high level of 4,000,000. Civil Rights measures and Bills to provide medical care for the aged had petered out in Congress for lack of leadership from the White House.

Richard Nixon and
Henry Cabot Lodge, the
Republican candidates for
the offices of President
and Vice-President
respectively.

John F. Kennedy

This was the record on which Nixon had to run for the Presidency in 1960, for disloyalty to Eisenhower would have been punished more than disloyalty to God. The result of the election, the narrow victory of the young Senator from Massachusetts, John Fitzgerald Kennedy, changed the rules of American politics. For the first time, Americans elected as their President a Roman Catholic of Irish stock and urban millionaire background in preference to a Protestant from a small town. The vote of the large cities and the Roman Catholics was decisive in the defeat of the countryside, which still distrusted immigrants and riches and cities and the Pope. As the white voters in the South shifted towards Republicanism – an alliance which would make the Republicans the party of conservatism – so the Democrats won progressive Republican support in rural areas. The American electorate began to be offered a choice between a conservative and a radical party instead of between four parties masquerading as two, when in fact each was split between its conservative and radical wings.

Although by 1960 Americans numbered only one in seventeen of the world's population, they consumed over half of the world's manufactured goods. They had become a nation of skilled workers employed by others;

John Fitzgerald Kennedy in Los Angeles on 1 November 1960, a week before he was elected President.

while only one in five Americans was not self-employed in 1800, now only one in eight was. For the first time, automation had allowed white-collar workers to outnumber blue-collar workers. High rates of pay had given many workers the chance to live in the style of the old middle classes of America. Seven in ten Americans now lived in urban or suburban areas, less than one in eight on farms. The population remained mobile; but the lines of migration had changed. These were no longer from East to West; but from the Deep South and the prairies out towards the coasts. California and Florida became the most expanding states in the Union.

The Quota System Immigration from overseas had been cut off since 1924 into the trickle of the quota system, although nearly a million aliens were allowed in after the Second World War as displaced persons or war brides. By 1950 more than nine Americans in ten were native-born. The closing of the gates to immigration explains to a certain extent why rural white Protestant fears of urban immigrant Catholics had subsided sufficiently to allow Kennedy's narrow victory in 1960. The proportion of Catholics to Protestants had remained at a constant ratio of one or two throughout the century, although the number of church-going Americans rose to three people in five by 1956. Officially, the majority of Americans had at last become godly, although the name of God was still not mentioned in the American Constitution.

The Americans not only could buy more goods than anyone else, they could also buy more life. The average white American could now expect to live for seventy years, twice the median age of Victorian times. The average working week declined from sixty to thirty-eight hours, while the personal spending power of industrial workers rose by more than one-half in the two decades after 1940. Once again, farm income suffered a relative decline, as it had in the 1920s, while the cities prospered. Or rather, while the suburbs prospered.

For the centres of the American cities were dying, as were the farms. Two-thirds of the 28,000,000 growth of the American people in the 1950s were absorbed by the new suburbs; one-quarter of all the houses lived in by Americans was built in the 1950s, mainly in the suburbs. Meanwhile, the centres of the great cities, those of Boston as well as San Francisco, of New York as well as Chicago, actually lost population. The grass prairies were pushing back the small farm while the asphalt prairies emptied the metropolis. More deer now roamed the United States than when the Pilgrims landed in the *Mayflower*.

The suburban sprawl.

Life in the suburbs had its problems. The rich present of two cars and a split-level house was bought on the future. One dollar in every nine of income was pledged to hire-purchase companies. The shift and growth of population were putting new strains on the schools. The United States had led the world in mass education, and, by 1960, there were nearly 35,000,000 students, while the university population was expected to double within ten years. Moreover, the demands of the new middle classes in the suburbs and of the new pattern of living changed many of the manufactures of American industry.

More cars and aeroplanes and oil products were needed to get the commuters from suburb to city, more electronic and electric machines to fill the demands of kitchen as well as defence budget. Chemicals and drugs were produced in huge quantities to look after the processing and packaging of food and the health and efficiency of consumers. The supermarket succeeded the general store, the garage and the airport cut back the livery stable and the railroad station. Between 1900 and 1930 the amount of electric power produced in the United States increased three times; by 1960 it had doubled again.

Two aspects of American life which have been adopted throughout the free world.

Good communica-
tions (*above*) and
ever-increasing auto-
mation (*left*) help
America to out-
produce any other
nation.

193

Soviet missiles bound for Cuba, November 1962.

An integrated government housing scheme.

A Civil Rights demonstration in Jackson, Mississippi.

The American economy changed too; tooth-and-claw competition gave way to a mixed economy. Various interacting forces dominated wages and prices; these forces included industry, business, banking, finance, organized labour, and agriculture. Each wanted a larger share of the national income and lobbied for it in Washington. The government, with its large concessions of tax rebates and defence contracts, kept the ring among the lobbies. The government was now the arbiter of the economy, if not the controller.

Yet although the majority of Americans were now wealthy, and although the first democracy of the rich in the world had been set up, some people still suffered. By 1960, one-eighth of all American families and one-third of all Negro families still lived on incomes which were barely at subsistence level. Not one of the children of the 500,000 migrant farm workers who still lived as the Okies had in the 1930s had ever been to a university. The bottom fifth of the American population only received one-twentieth of the national income. The gap between rich and poor was still great in the land of opportunity, and that opportunity was depending more and more on inherited rather than acquired wealth.

It was to meet these needs and stresses in American society that Kennedy promised his New Frontier of 'unknown opportunities and perils' to complete the New Freedom and the New Deals. But Congress proved hostile and put down roadblocks as bristling as British colonial guardposts to contain the expansion of the New Frontier. Kennedy failed to push through Bills *The New Frontier*

The scene in Dallas, Texas, a few moments after President Kennedy was assassinated on 22 November 1963.

asking for aid for education, a higher minimum wage, and free health care for the one American in twelve who was an old person. He only won a federal housing bill, a large defence budget, and room to negotiate tariff cuts. His head-on battle with the large steel companies, to prevent them from raising prices, made big business wary of him, and his use of federal troops to protect a Negro student at the University of Mississippi alienated the South.

Kennedy's greatest success was in foreign policy. After the fiasco of supporting the rebel invasion of Cuba at the Bay of Pigs, a scheme inherited from Eisenhower, he later forced the Russians to remove their clandestine rocket bases from the island at the risk of nuclear war. The result was that the Democrats did well in the elections of 1962, although the Party in power normally does badly in mid-term elections. Nixon, nosed out of the White House, was even defeated in his attempt to become Governor of California.

The year before Kennedy's assassination at Dallas was a year of stalemate. The Senate seemed determined to thwart the will of the President, who had only been a junior Senator himself. All his measures for cutting taxes and increasing Civil Rights were held up, while Negro militance grew. In foreign policy, however, tensions between America and Russia eased, because of Russia's growing rift with China. The Alliance for Progress in Latin America and the Peace Corps were also moderately successful.

Lyndon Johnson The murder of Kennedy in Texas did not bring about a wave of conservative nationalism, as it might well have done. Vice-President Lyndon Johnson quickly dispelled fears of his brash Texan ranching style by his caution in the White House and his support of the Kennedy programme still waterlogged in Congress. His deliberate appeal to all moderates in American society soon gave him great popular backing. His inner knowledge of the workings of the Senate, where he had been Democratic Majority Leader, had taught him how to bully and manage Bills through to laws, while his public image as the great persuader was built up by his call for a consensus and for reasoning together. He kept to the middle of the road as carefully as an Eisenhower; but his view of where that middle lay showed a Democratic bias. He pruned the budget, trimmed foreign aid, and went in for the government economy so dear to the American people; but he saw the time had come for the advance of the Negroes and for aid to the poor. Only in foreign policy did he prefer the use of power to persuasion, particularly in South Vietnam, where United States policy began to slide from aid to intervention and full-scale war.

President Johnson.

Barry Goldwater.

When the Republicans nominated Senator Barry Goldwater for the Presidency in 1964, they set a seal on the revolution in American politics. Goldwater would rather be far right than President and he ran his campaign that way. Moderate Republicans were left to sink or swim as best they could in state or congressional elections; most sank under the flood of Democratic votes which beached Johnson in the White House with a margin great enough to make him feel complacent.

Goldwater, who carried only five states in the Deep South and his home state of Arizona, was damned by seeming a warmonger, a trigger-happy hip-shooter. In fact, his most belligerent policy was a call to bomb North Vietnam – a policy that Johnson adopted immediately after his victory. Yet Goldwater was the devoted friend of big business; his election would have put the clock back to a rural time almost before clocks. His massive repudiation showed that the American people disliked excessive conservatism as much as they disliked excessive radicalism; urban and industrial America now dominated the old taboos against federal power and pressure on the individual.

Oil dumps, 45 miles from Hanoi, being bombed by planes from a carrier of the United States Seventh Fleet, 1966.

Civil Rights demonstrators in Chicago (*left*) and the start of the Selma march (*right*). Dr Martin Luther King is in the foreground centre of the second photograph.

Two revolutions had bound the United States inextricably into the web of the world, the revolution in communications and in war. Another invasion of Cuba by the Americans might begin an atomic Armageddon. One continent, the Americas, could not regulate its own affairs without involving the world. The breakthrough in communications that had united the United States had bound it to the United Nations. The Atlantic and the Pacific had become no greater barriers to nuclear destruction than the Rhine or the Don. When America accepted Alaska and Hawaii as members of the United States, it accepted that natural frontiers no longer had a meaning and that outposts of America could exist beyond the seas.

New defence needs created new problems in civil government. Some suspected the military establishment in the Pentagon of directing policy, despite the control of the powerful Secretary of Defence, Robert McNamara; others feared that disarmament would be impossible because defence spending was needed to keep the economy healthy. Yet Kennedy did succeed in signing a ban on nuclear testing above the ground, and even after the fall of Khrushchev, relations between America and Russia remained polite, if cool.

Robert McNamara.

Although Johnson decided on a foreign policy of limited force, including old-style intervention in the Dominican Republic, fear of Mao Tse-tung seemed likely to keep the uneasy truce between the United States and Russia.

At home, Johnson's skill with Congress led to vast successes in his plans for a Great Society. He began to clear up some of the anomalies in America, such as the lack of opportunity of the very poor, the waste of natural resources, the wrecking of the landscape, the bad treatment of immigrants, and the exclusion of Catholic schools from educational aid. Negroes were given more economic opportunity and votes in the South; old people received free medical care. Johnson suited America particularly well, for he had the city mind of the tycoon allied with a country style and heart.

The American
Way of Life
The nation, too, has an urban skin and a rural conscience. Most of the stresses in American life, the high rate of crime and violence and delinquency and divorce, the cruelty of men to men and their slavery to machines and organizations, come from too rapid a change from village to megalopolis. City and suburban life still seem unnatural. Washington itself was only a country town sixty years ago; it is now the capital of half the globe and the southern end of a vast hive of 40,000,000 people who live in one city stretching 400 miles along that barren coast which faced the Pilgrims only 350 years before.

The American population now approaches 200,000,000 and lives mainly in or near cities. Yet many characteristics remain those which de Tocqueville noticed in the 1830s; many American traditions deny a modern urban environment. De Tocqueville noted a maxim 'that everyone is the best and sole judge of his own private interest, and that society has no right to control a man's actions.' This ethic of the wilderness obviously has little place now in a suburban society where community actions are important. Yet it persists with the consequences that de Tocqueville perceived, 'gross instances of social indifference and neglect', although these instances are due less to callous behaviour than to a belief that men should help themselves. The fact that heredity makes some people unfit to help themselves is taking a long time to be recognized generally in the land of the free.

De Tocqueville saw another illuminating facet of American life. Society there seemed to him 'to live from hand to mouth, like an army in the field'. The makeshift habit of Americans, their ability to construct at speed and their capacity for waste, has endured in the quick replacement of things.

Christmas rush-hour in New York. ▶

The skyscrapers of New York are sometimes built with a life expectancy of twenty years; Manhattan Island, in living and construction, is the world's first perpetual motion machine. Houses as well as cars now include planned defects of obsolescence. The rapid deterioration of things will mean continuous unnecessary work for future generations.

For leisure is still something of a sin in the United States; any work, even superfluous work, seems better. To be paid for doing nothing is still too revolutionary a concept for the wealthiest society in the world. As a result, middle-class Americans are now living in less solid houses and often eat less well than their grandfathers. They are doing so because they have converted habits of industry and speed, once necessary to exploit the resources of a continent, into fetishes which hamper them from enjoying their rich civilization.

Since the Romans, however, no nation has produced such miracles of communications and engineering, the marvels of their age. American highways, like the Roman military roads, span and partition the continent. And the great American bridges surpass the seven wonders of the world. There are few more remarkable men in history than O. H. Ammann, the builder of the George Washington Bridge, who, at the age of eighty, designed and built the Verrazano Narrows Bridge, the skeleton wings of which hang as an embalmed bird of passage before the inlet to New York. The skyscrapers, too, of Manhattan Island stand not unlike the Tower of Babel, and every city of the earth has learned to build towards the sky after the American example. The Romans pioneered the road and the sewer; the Americans have created the big bridge and the tall block.

De Tocqueville also observed that there was no country in which there was 'so little true independence of mind and freedom of discussion as in America'. But there was a reason for this state of affairs. The immigrant to America had an urgent desire to accept current morality in order to be accepted in his turn as a new American. His sailing across the Atlantic was an act of repudiation of Europe and the past, his landing in the New World a readiness to believe in what the New World believed. But the effective ending of mass immigration from Europe in 1924 has turned this immigrant desire to become American as soon as possible into a contagious need to show oneself as American as everyone else. The ideal of loving one's neighbour has become the social duty of living like him. The wish to cherish one's friends has turned into the desire to consume what they consume.

Golden Gate Bridge, San Francisco, looking north. ▶

Saul Bellow.

J. D. Salinger.

It has been the measure of American greatness to melt together a polyglot people and to conquer a continent in a matter of seventy years. But now that nature has been largely conquered, the drives of the past remain only as the taboos of the future. Conformity is now no longer a need since the United States has discovered a fierce national identity; what is wanted is to preserve the diversity of the American traditions of mountain and prairie and seaboard and desert and ghetto. To conform was once an urgent faith in proclaiming oneself a good American. This creed has been used by advertisers to make Americans desire the same brands of goods.

Urban fact is destroying tradition and rural myth. American literature points to the trend. The great writers of Anglo-Saxon rural virtue and rural vice, Hemingway and Faulkner, are dead; the writers rising to take their place, such as Saul Bellow and J. D. Salinger, are city-bred sons of immigrant parents. The rural school of critics is also losing influence; the Southern critics are being pushed into the backwoods by the American-Jewish urban critics, the heirs of Lionel Trilling. Even Robert Lowell, the leading American poet, comes from an urban, if traditional family, and mirrors the pressures and conflicts of city existence.

The virulent reaction against the myth of rural virtue by Mencken in the 1920s has given way to the dominant and tempered praise of the urban scene by urban people. Nostalgic nineteenth-century portraits of life at the swimming-hole or in the barn are now being replaced by sweet-sour modern reminiscences of life in the Bronx ghetto or the tenement slum. There is no need now for a tree to grow in Brooklyn to hallow the immigrant novel as part of the new American literature. Brooklyn needs only its bricks. In fact, the country has now taken the city's place as the home of literary evil, with rape and incest and lynching the apparent daily bread of the Deep South. The slum is now the home of *kitsch* and kisses and rich private life. Once politicians had to be born in a log-cabin; now they need to be cradled in a millionaire's mansion or a tenement block.

Perhaps nothing shows the domination of the new city more than the fact that New York has taken over from Paris as the centre of modern art. Jackson Pollock and his abstract successors have done for the art world of Manhattan what the Impressionists did at the end of the nineteenth century for the Left Bank. Abstract art broke up the traditional American school of inferior rural paintings and gave a picture of the fragmentation of modern urban existence. For two decades now, city values have dominated the artist's vision, values of advertising or cinema or optical illusion. Eden is no longer the source of the creator's inspiration; he has come to accept and draw inspiration from the Babylon which is his home and his market.

Although the character of the American people has remained remarkably constant, as mobile and pragmatic and hard-working and materialistic as ever, its change-over to urban life and to urban goods and evils has produced stress and strain on its traditional patterns of existence. The fact that one marriage in four now ends in divorce and that psychoanalysis has replaced neighbourliness as the relief of the unhappy shows that the old morality of the farm has not grown into the new one of the street. The suburb has not had time to set down roots.

Technological change has briefly outstripped social change. The inventions of the cheap car and the cheap contraceptive have outrun the snail's pace of moral evolution. Eisenhower might find himself chosen to be responsible for the complex political decisions of a hemisphere, but he could not escape the black-and-white choices, the simple creed of rights and wrongs, of the small town in Kansas where he was brought up. America has grown rich and international too fast for many of its people and some of its leaders. There has been no London or Paris with a traditoin of centuries to provide a natural way of life among bricks and mortar. As Henry Steel Commager has commented, American civilization has become urban, but it is not yet an urbane civilization.

What has changed since the time of de Tocqueville is the growing role of the government in the United States, a process denounced by the right wing of the Republican Party as 'creeping socialism'. De Tocqueville wrote accurately in the 1830s that the federal government was the exception, while the government of the states was the rule. As late as 1900 the federal budget was only half a billion dollars a year, much less than the present budget of New York State. The whole office staff of the White House under President McKinley was six people and four doorkeepers and messengers; it now exceeds two thousand. And the government of the states is now the exception, the federal government the rule.

The Americans have invented things faster than they have adapted themselves to the things they have invented. They have put up, for the first time, a skein of cities across a continent; they even propose to water the Great American Desert by tapping the snows of Alaska 2000 miles away. If the vitality of their doing often appears raw, it is the mere rudeness left over from the recent conquest of nature. If their civilization appears materialistic, it is because things have to be tamed before people may put their souls within them. If American capitalism appears crude, it is because a people has developed a continent in a mere seventy years, making itself wealthy more swiftly then any people at any time. To reach an El Dorado for the masses and to reject it is not possible for human-kind, especially as the dream of El Dorado brought most immigrants to the New World in the first place.

Yet now that the Americans have an empire of things, they are turning to put their jerry-built palace in order. Their economy is now mixed, not naked in its capitalism. They have admitted their interdependence with the rest of the human race, even if their present foreign policy is based on the big stick and the big carrot rather than on the big brother. They are making efforts to reach an agreement with Communism before a nuclear war destroys both ways of life. The frightening power of technology has brought modera-tion to American affairs.

As Mr Dooley once observed of America, the noise to be heard there was not the first gun of a revolution. It was only the people of the United States beating a carpet during a bout of national house-cleaning. To them, quick change was short change. Acceptable reform has to come slowly through conviction, even though technological change has come fast. It has always been the way of the Americans to invent a new corkscrew rather than a better society, in the hope that the first may open the way to the second. Their pioneering in space may well lead to greater things.

California and Arizona photographed from space. ▶

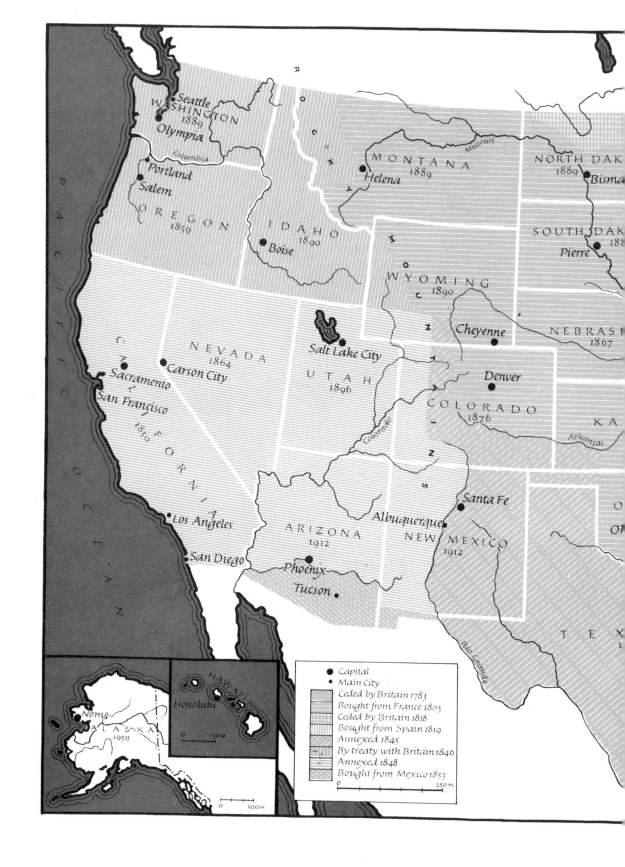

Seattle
WASHINGTON
1889
Olympia

Portland
Salem

Columbia

R
O
C

MONTANA
1889
Helena

Missouri

NORTH DAK
1889
Bisma

OREGON
1859

IDAHO
1890
Boise

SOUTH DAK
188

Pierre

WYOMING
1890

Cheyenne

NEBRAS
1867

N E V A D A
1864
Carson City

C
A
L
I
F
O
R
N
I
A

1850

Sacramento
San Francisco

Salt Lake City

U T A H
1896

Denver

COLORADO
1876

KA

Arkansas

Colorado

Los Angeles

San Diego

A R I Z O N A
1912

Phoenix
Tucson

Albuquerque

Santa Fe

NEW MEXICO
1912

O

OK

T E X
I

P
A
C
I
F
I
C

O
C
E
A
N

Rio Grande

Nome

ALASKA
1959

HAWAII 1900

Honolulu

0   150 M.

- Capital
• Main City

Ceded by Britain 1783
Bought from France 1803
Ceded by Britain 1818
Bought from Spain 1819
Annexed 1845
By treaty with Britain 1846
Annexed 1848
Bought from Mexico 1853

0   250 M.

0   300 M.

Suggestions for Further Reading

GENERAL

Boorstin, D.J., *The Genius of American Politics* (1953).

Brogan, D.W., *The American Political System* (1933).

Commager, H.S., *The American Mind* (1960).

Curti, M.E., *The Growth of American Thought* (3rd ed., 1964).

Degler, C.N., *Out of Our Past: The Forces that Shaped Modern America* (1959).

Handlin, O., *The American People* (1963).

—, *Race and Nationality in American Life* (1958).

Hofstadter, R., *The American Political Tradition and the Men Who Made It* (1948).

Miller, W., *A New History of the United States* (1958).

Parrington, V.L., *Main Currents in American Thought* (3 vols., 1927-30).

Potter, D.M., *People of Plenty* (1954).

THE COLONIAL PERIOD

Bridenbaugh, C., *Cities in Revolt: Urban Life in America, 1743–1776* (1955).

Crèvecoeur, H. St J. de, *Letters from an American Farmer* (1782).

DeVoto, B., *The Course of Empire* (1952).

Jones, H.M., *O Strange New World* (1964).

Miller, P., *The New England Mind* (2 vols., 1953).

Morison, S.E., *The Intellectual Life of Colonial New England* (2nd ed., 1956).

Osgood, H.L., *The American Colonies in the Eighteenth Century* (1924).

Sweet, W.W., *The Story of Religion in America* (1950).

THE AMERICAN REVOLUTION
AND THE VIRGINIA DYNASTY

Alden, J.R., *The American Revolution* (1954).

Allen, H.C., *Great Britain and the United States* (1954).

Beard, C.A., *An Economic Interpretation of the Constitution of the United States* (1935).

Becker, C.L., *The Declaration of Independence* (1922).

Binkley, W.E. and Moos, M., *A Grammar of American Politics* (1950).

Chinard, G., *Thomas Jefferson, the Apostle of Americanism* (1957).

Cunliffe, M., *George Washington: Man and Monument* (1959).

Gipson, L.H., *The Coming of the Revolution, 1765–1775* (1954).

Jensen, M., *The New Nation, 1781–1789* (1950).

Knollenberg, B., *Origins of the American Revolution, 1759–1766* (1960).

Nye, R.B., *The Cultural Life of the New Nation, 1776–1830* (1960).

Peterson, M.D., *The Jefferson Image in the American Mind* (1960).

Rossiter, C.L. (editor), *The Federalist Papers* (1961).

Schachner, N., *Alexander Hamilton* (1946).

Wright, E., *Fabric of Freedom, 1763–1800* (1961).

WESTWARD EXPANSION

Billington, R.A., *Westward Expansion: A History of the American Frontier* (2nd ed., 1960).

Graebner, N.A., *Empire on the Pacific* (1955).

Merk, F., *Manifest Destiny and Mission in American History* (1963).

Smith, H.N., *Virgin Land: The American West as Symbol and Myth* (1950).

Turner, F.J., *The Frontier in American History* (1920).

—, *The Significance of Sections in American History* (1932).

Wade, R.C., *The Urban Frontier: The Rise of Western Cities, 1790–1830* (1959).

Webb, W.P., *The Great Plains* (1931).

THE COMING OF DEMOCRACY

Burlingame, R., *March of the Iron Men* (1938).

Dangerfield, G., *The Era of Good Feelings* (1953).

Filler, L., *The Crusade Against Slavery, 1830–1860* (1960).

Hammond, B., *Banks and Politics in America from the Revolution to the Civil War* (1958).

Meyers, M., *The Jacksonian Persuasion: Politics and Belief* (1958).

Probst, G.E. (editor), *The Happy Republic* (1962).

Schlesinger, A.M., Jr, *The Age of Jackson* (1947).

Sinclair, A., *Prohibition: The Era of Excess* (1962).

—, *The Better Half* (1965).

de Tocqueville, C.A.H.C., *Democracy in America* (2 vols., 1835).

Tyler, A.F., *Freedom's Ferment* (1944).

Ward, J.W., *Andrew Jackson, Symbol for an Age* (1955).

CIVIL WAR, RECONSTRUCTION
AND REUNION

Buck, P.H., *The Road to Reunion, 1865–1900* (1947).

Cash, W.J., *The Mind of the South* (1941).

Craven, A., *The Coming of the Civil War* (2nd ed., 1957).

Franklin, J.H., *Reconstruction after the Civil War* (1961).

Myrdal, G., *An American Dilemma* (2 vols., 1944).

Nevins, A., *Ordeal of the Union* (2 vols., 1947).

—, *The Emergence of Lincoln* (2 vols., 1950).

Nye, R.B., *Fettered Freedom* (rev. ed., 1963).

Olmstead, F.L., *The Cotton Kingdom* (1861).

Simkins, F.B., *A History of the South* (1958).

Stampp, K., *The Peculiar Institution: Slavery in the Ante-Bellum South* (1956).

Thomas, B.P., *Abraham Lincoln* (1953).

Woodward, C.V., *Origins of the New South, 1877–1913* (1951).

INDUSTRIALISM AND REFORM

Blum, J.M., *The Republican Roosevelt* (1954).

Bryce, J., *The American Commonwealth* (2 vols., 1888).

Burlingame, R., *Engines of Democracy* (1940).

Dunne, F.P., *Mr. Dooley at His Best* (1938).

Faulkner, H.U., *The Decline of Laissez-Faire* (1951).

Goldman, E.F., *Rendezvous with Destiny* (1952).

Handlin, O., *The Uprooted* (1951).

Hicks, J.D., *The Populist Revolt* (1931).

Higham, J., *Strangers in the Land: Patterns of American Nativism, 1860–1925* (1955).

Hofstadter, R., *Social Darwinism in American Thought* (rev. ed., 1959).

—, *The Age of Reform: From Bryan to F.D.R.* (1955).

Jones, M.A., *American Immigration* (1960).

Link, A.S., *Woodrow Wilson and the Progressive Era, 1910–1917* (1954).

Mowry, G.E., *The Era of Theodore Roosevelt, 1900–1912* (1958).

Veblen, T.B., *The Theory of the Leisure Class* (1899).

CONSTITUTIONAL, DIPLOMATIC
AND ADMINISTRATIVE HISTORY

Bailey, T.A., *A Diplomatic History of the American People* (rev. ed., 1955).

McCloskey, R.G., *The American Supreme Court* (1960).

Swisher, C.B., *Growth of Constitutional Power in the United States* (rev. ed., 1954).

White, L.D., *The Federalists: A Study in Administrative History* (1956).

—, *The Jeffersonians* (1951).

—, *The Jacksonians* (1954)

—, *The Republican Era, 1869–1901* (1958).

WORLD POWER

Allen, F.L., *Only Yesterday* (1931).

Burns, J.M., *Roosevelt, the Lion and the Fox* (1956).

Cochran, T.C. and Miller, W., *The Age of Enterprise: A Social History of Industrial America* (1942).

Freidel, F., *Franklin D. Roosevelt* (3 vols., 1952–6).

Galbraith, J.K., *The Affluent Society* (1958).

—, *American Capitalism: The Concept of Countervailing Power* (1952).

—, *The Great Crash, 1929* (1955).

Glazer N. and Moynihan, D.P., *Beyond the Melting-Pot* (1963).

Leuchtenburg, W., *The Perils of Prosperity, 1914–1932* (1958).

—, *Franklin D. Roosevelt and the New Deal, 1932–40* (1963).

Lubell, S., *The Future of American Politics* (1952).

Lynd, H.M. and R.S., *Middletown* (1929).

Riesman, D., *The Lonely Crowd* (1950).

Rovere, R.H., *Senator Joe McCarthy* (1960).

Schlesinger, A.M., Jr, *The Age of Roosevelt* (3 vols., 1957–61).

White, T.H., *The Making of the President 1960* (1961).

List of Illustrations

Index

Date Due

NOV 8 '68	FEB 2 '73	
DEC 3 '68	FEB 19 '74	
FEB 1 '69	MAY 12 '78	
MAR 12 '69		
NOV 12 '69		
DEC 18 '69		
JAN 8 '70		
MAY 6 '70		
NOV 19 '71		
DEC 7 '71		
JAN 7 '72		